Thus, the task is not so much to see
what no one yet has seen,
but to think what nobody yet has thought
about that which everybody sees.

Schopenhauer

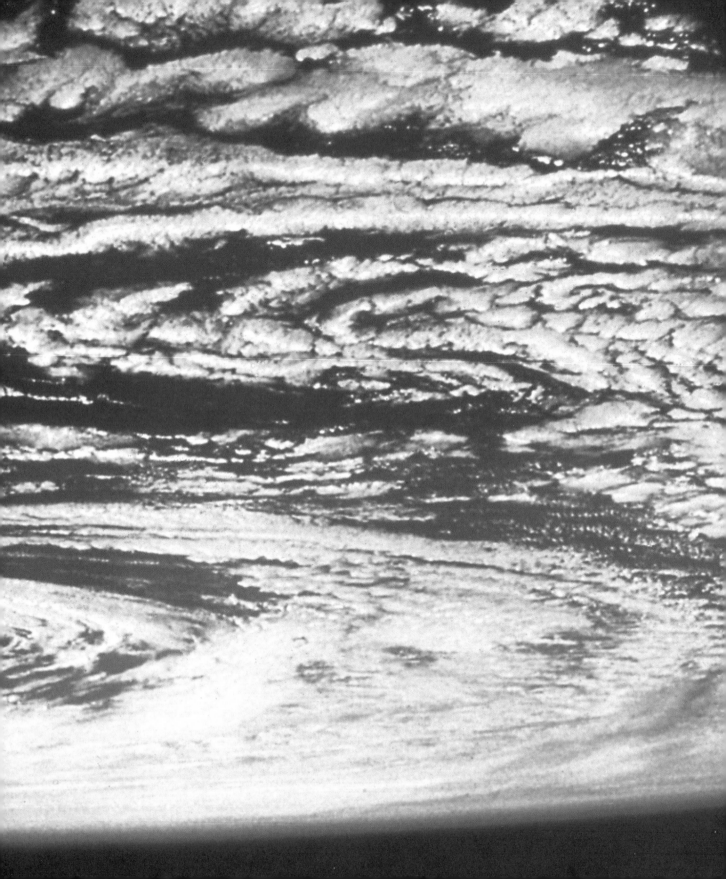

a simpler way

Margaret J. Wheatley

Myron Kellner-Rogers

Berrett-Koehler Publishers
San Francisco

Berrett-Koehler Publishers, Inc.
155 Montgomery Street
San Francisco, CA 94104-4109
Tel: (415) 288-0260 Fax: (415) 362-2512

Ordering Information

Individual sales. Berrett-Koehler publications are available through most bookstores. They can also be ordered direct from Berrett-Koehler at the address above.

Quantity sales. Special discounts are available on quantity purchases by corporations, associations, and others. For details, contact the "Special Sales Department" at the Berrett-Koehler address above.

Orders for college textbook/course adoption use. Please contact Berrett-Koehler Publishers at the address above.

Orders by U.S. trade bookstores and wholesalers. Please contact Publishers Group West, 4065 Hollis Street, Box 8843, Emeryville, CA 94662. Tel: (510) 658-3453; 1-800-788-3123. Fax: (510) 658-1834

Design by Adrian Pulfer and Jeff Streeper
Production by David Meredith
Printed in the United States of America

Library of Congress Cataloging-in-Publication Data

Wheatley, Margaret J.
     A simpler way/Margaret J. Wheatley, Myron Kellner-Rogers.
       p. cm.
     Includes bibliographical references and index.
     ISBN 1-881052-95-8 (alk paper)
     1. Life   2. Organization   3. Play (Philosophy)   4. Evolution
I. Kellner-Rogers, Myron, 1952-   II. Title.
BD435.W46 1996
128--dc20
                                        96-15999
                                           CIP

First Edition July 1996
99 98 97 96   10 9 8 7 6 5 4 3 2 1

for all of us

Some go first, and others come long afterward.
God blesses both and all in the line,
and replaces what has been consumed,
and provides for those who work the soil of helpfulness. . .

Jelaluddin Rumi
13th century Persia

contents

an invitation

We want life to be less arduous and more delightful.

We want to be able to think differently about how to organize human activities.

This book springs from these desires. It explores a different way of thinking about life and about how organizing activities might occur. It is grounded in our beliefs, our experiences, and our hopes. It represents our present understandings and our most intriguing questions. It is an expression of what we have learned and what we hope to discover.

The mechanistic image of the world is a very deep image, planted at subterranean depths in most of us. But it doesn't help us any longer. Our own search for new ways of understanding has led us to philosophers, scientists, poets, novelists, spiritual teachers, colleagues, audiences, and each other. We keep exploring what we can see when we look at life and organizations using different images.

The primary question of this book is: How could we organize human endeavor if we developed different understandings of how life organizes itself?

As authors, we ask this question for all of us, for there is no one who lives life unaffected by the organizations we have created. And we invite each of you into the inquiry. We hope we have succeeded in creating a work that evokes your own experience and connection with the concepts we describe. We want the design and arrangement of this book to invite you into new ways of seeing. We all need one other to explore these ideas. Each of us contributes our experiences and thinking to one another as we try to understand the world differently. We are essential to each other's inquiry. We welcome you.

As we have played with new ideas and a new worldview, we keep attending to our beliefs. So much of human behavior is habitual. And behind every habit is a belief – about people, life, the world. We work from the premise that if we can know our beliefs, we can then act with greater consciousness about our behaviors. Examining beliefs has become a compelling process for us (and probably has made us annoying to more people than we care to account for).

Here are our present beliefs about human organizations and the world in which they come into form.

The universe is a living, creative, experimenting experience of discovering what's possible at all levels of scale, from microbe to cosmos.

Life's natural tendency is to organize. Life organizes into greater levels of complexity to support more diversity and greater sustainability.

Life organizes around a self. Organizing is always an act of creating an identity.

Life self-organizes. Networks, patterns, and structures emerge without external imposition or direction. Organization wants to happen.

People are intelligent, creative, adaptive, self-organizing, and meaning-seeking.

Organizations are living systems. They too are intelligent, creative, adaptive, self-organizing, meaning-seeking.

These beliefs are ours. They have emerged from the kinds of information and perspectives that are included in this book. You may develop different beliefs as you read. We encourage you to question yourself at the level of your beliefs. Such personal questioning requires us to go very deeply into our ideas about the world. It often causes us to challenge more than we want to have challenged. But we have found that belief is the place from which true change originates. Belief is why we have written this book.

a simpler way

There is a simpler way to organize human endeavor. It requires a new way of being in the world. It requires being in the world without fear. Being in the world with play and creativity. Seeking after what's possible. Being willing to learn and to be surprised.

This simpler way to organize human endeavor requires a belief that the world is inherently orderly. The world seeks organization. It does not need us humans to organize it.

This simpler way summons forth what is best about us. It asks us to understand human nature differently, more optimistically. It identifies us as creative. It acknowledges that we seek after meaning. It asks us to be less serious, yet more purposeful, about our work and our lives. It does not separate play from the nature of being.

This world of a simpler way is a world we already know. We may not have seen it clearly, but we have been living in it all our lives. It is a world that is more welcoming, more hospitable to our humanness. Who we are and what is best about us can more easily flourish.

The world we had been taught to see was alien to our humanness. We were taught to see the world as a great machine. But then we could find nothing human in it. Our thinking grew even stranger – we turned this world-image back on ourselves and believed that we too were machines.

Because we could not find ourselves in the machine world we had created in thought, we experienced the world as foreign and fearsome. Alienation spawned the need to dominate. Fear led to control. We wanted to harness and control everything. We tried, but it did not stop the fear. Mistakes threatened us; failed plans ruined us; relentless mechanistic forces demanded absolute submission. There was little room for human concerns.

But the world is not a machine. It is alive, filled with life and the history of life. Whatever ancient rocks we discover, notes biologist James Lovelock, we also discover ancient life preserved in them. Life cannot be eradicated from the world, even though our metaphors have tried.

As we change our images of the world, as we leave behind the machine, we welcome ourselves back. We recover a world that is supportive of human endeavor.

This world of a simpler way has a natural and spontaneous tendency toward organization. It seeks order. Whatever chaos is present at the start, when elements combine, systems of organization appear. Life is attracted to order – order gained through wandering explorations into new relationships and new possibilities.

In this world, we can move with more assurance. The world supports our efforts more than we could have hoped. We can create, experiment, organize, fail, accomplish, play, learn, create again.

It is life's invitation to freedom, creativity, and meaning that welcomes us back. These are the desires of human existence. Now we can see our reflection in the world. It is we humans, says physicist Ilya Prigogine, who are "the most striking realization of the basic laws of nature."

If we can be in the world in the fullness of our humanity, what are we capable of? If we are free to play, to experiment and discover, if we are free to fail, what might we create? What could we accomplish if we stopped trying to structure the world into existence? What could we accomplish if we worked with life's natural tendency to organize? Who could we be if we found a simpler way?

poetics

A. R. Ammons

I look for the way
things will turn
out spiralling from a center,
the shape
things will take to come forth in

so that the birch tree white
touched black at branches
will stand out
wind-glittering
totally its apparent self:

I look for the forms
things want to come as

from what black wells of possibility,
how a thing will
unfold:

not the shape on paper – though
that, too – but the
uninterfering means on paper:

not so much looking for the shape
as being available
to any shape that may be
summoning itself
through me
from the self not mine but ours.

play

I look for the way
things will turn
out spiralling from a center

Life is creative. It plays itself into existence, seeking out new relationships, new capacities, new traits. Life is an experiment to discover what's possible. As it tinkers with discovery, it creates more and more possibilities. With so much freedom for discovery, how can life be anything but playful?

What has kept us from seeing life as creative, even playful? At least since Darwin, Western culture has harbored some great errors. We have believed that the world is hostile, that we are in a constant struggle for survival, that the consequence of error is death, that the environment seeks our destruction. In such a world, there is no safety. Who wouldn't be afraid?

Darwinistic thought solidified the belief that life was not supposed to happen. Life was an accident, just one of many random events. Because the world had never intended for life to appear, the world had no obligation to sustain it. Life had to fight for every breath, tested constantly by an unwelcoming and unforgiving environment. Species appeared by chance. Individuals that stumbled on lucky genetic errors survived. The environment loomed over every living thing, ready to challenge, ready to destroy. It was an awesome responsibility life faced: Get it right, or die.

These errors of thought have guided most of our decisions. They have kept us from seeing a world which is continuously exploring and creating. Life is about invention, not survival. We are here to create, not to defend. Out beyond the shadows of Darwinistic thought, a wholly different world appears. A world that delights in its explorations. A world that makes it up as it goes along. A world that welcomes us into the exploration as good partners.

Images of life as creative and playful have been with us for thousands of years in many spiritual traditions, but modern Western thought makes it difficult to approach life as play. As writers inviting you to think about what human life could be if we all saw the world as playful and creative, we have chosen to weave one poem through our work. This is not just because we love poetry but also because, in a creative and playful world, all of us are, all the time, poets.

All of us are always engaged in trying to convey our experience of life in images that can connect it with other experiences. Even the most analytic science, the most careful construction of models, is always poetry, the creation of images that evoke experience, linking things together for new ways of comprehending. We cannot know the world in an objective way. We can never get outside our senses to determine if reality exists in some sphere beyond us. We can never gain a true picture of how it really is. We can never observe what's "right."

We peer out through our senses, describing our experience of what we think reality to be. We choose images to convey our experience. We create metaphors to connect what we see. We explore new ways of understanding what seems to be happening and what we think it means.

Ezra Pound called poetry "the language of exploration." The place to begin our exploration of a creative, playful world is with the acknowledgment that we are all poets, exploring possibilities of meaning in a world which is also all the time exploring possibilities.

"I believe I experience creativity at every moment of my life," said French philosopher Henri Bergson. Can our own lives be such joyous experiences? Perhaps we can move into this experience by understanding how life creates itself. Life's process of creating is quite different from what we had thought. There are enough underlying principles to this process that we could call it a logic, a logic of play. In fact, we would like to call it the logic of life. The key elements of this logic are evident in recent work by scientists that explore how life comes into being.

Everything is in a constant process of discovery and creating. Everything is changing all the time: individuals, systems, environments, the rules, the processes of evolution. Even change changes. Every organism reinterprets the rules, creates exceptions for itself, creates new rules.

Life uses messes to get to well-ordered solutions. Life doesn't seem to share our desires for efficiency or neatness. It uses redundancy, fuzziness, dense webs of relationships, and unending trials and errors to find what works.

Life is intent on finding what works, not what's "right." It is the ability to keep finding solutions that is important; any one solution is temporary. There are no permanently right answers. The capacity to keep changing, to find what works now, is what keeps any organism alive.

Life creates more possibilities as it engages with opportunities. There are no "windows of opportunity," narrow openings in the fabric of space-time that soon disappear forever. Possibilities beget more possibilities; they are infinite.

Life is attracted to order. It experiments until it discovers how to form a system that can support diverse members. Individuals search out a wide range of possible relationships to discover whether they can organize into a life-sustaining system. These explorations continue until a system is discovered. This system then provides stability for its members, so that individuals are less buffeted by change.

Life organizes around identity. Every living thing acts to develop and preserve itself. Identity is the filter that every organism or system uses to make sense of the world. New information, new relationships, changing environments – all are interpreted through a sense of self. This tendency toward self-creation is so strong that it creates a seeming paradox. An organism will change to maintain its identity.

Everything participates in the creation and evolution of its neighbors. There are no unaffected outsiders. No one system dictates conditions to another. All participate together in creating the conditions of their interdependence.

Life is creative. It makes it up as it goes along, changing the rules even. This behavior flies in the face of the logic we inherited about how the world works. Most of us grew up in a world where we believed things existed in a fixed and independent state. Things could be understood by analysis. Laws and principles could be extracted from observations of their behavior. Predictions could be made for similar situations. Right answers would be hard won by bright minds. Safety would be earned by assiduous analysis.

We have focused for a long time on trying to discover what's right. We have taken things apart, sifting through our analysis for the right answer, creating more and more debris, surrounded by numbers that overwhelm us with dissatisfactions.

These activities are cloaked in terror. What if we don't find it? What if we get it wrong? What if someone else finds it before we do? Extinction will follow swiftly on the heels of any mistake. This fear of error seems the darkest of Darwinian shadows. When errors hold so much peril, play disappears. Creativity ceases. Only fear and struggle persist. Paradoxically, we make greater errors.

We say to one another, "Get it right the first time." How can we live with so much fear?

There is no such thing as survival of the fittest, only survival of the fit. This means that there is no one answer that is right, but many answers that might work. Life explores all sorts of combinations, content to find anything that works.

The puzzle in biology is not how natural selection forces an organism into one right solution. The puzzle is how so much diversity, such rampant profligacy, can be tamed sufficiently to develop organisms that are similar enough to reproduce. Why are there so many different plants and animals? Perhaps it is because life has only these simple criteria: Whatever you become, make sure you can survive and reproduce. These are very broad constraints, not strict rules. Given so much freedom, organisms take off in all directions, exploring what's possible.

Nature encourages wild self-expression as long as it doesn't threaten the survival of the organism. The world supports incredible levels of diversity, playful additions to one's physical appearance, unique excursions into color and flair. There is no ideal design for anything, just interesting combinations that arise as a living thing explores its space of possibilities.

Yet we have terrorized ourselves as a species by the thought of evolution, driving ourselves into positions of paralyzing conformity for fear of getting things wrong.

This world of wild exploration is one which tinkers itself into existence. A French biologist describes the process of creating living things as *bricolage* – assembling parts and items in complicated arrangements, not because they fit some ideal design, but just because they are possible.

Tinkerers have skills but no clear plans. They make do with the materials at hand. Does such tinkering make life appear indifferent, relativistic, crassly opportunistic? Or does it reveal life's delight in exploration, in discovering what's possible? Tinkering opens us to what's possible in the moment. Analytic plans drive us only toward what we think we already know.

But life's tinkering has direction. It tinkers toward order – toward systems that are more complex and more effective. The process used is exploratory and messy, but the movement is toward order. In human attempts to construct functioning ecosystems, scientists cannot predict what will work. But they do know that the system will seek stability. Almost always, what begins in randomness ends in stability. Life seeks solutions, tends toward support and stability, generates systems that sustain diverse individuals. Life is attracted to order.

But how it gets there violates all of our rules of good process: Life is not neat, parsimonious, logical, nor elegant. Life seeks order in a disorderly way. Life uses processes we find hard to tolerate and hard to believe in – mess upon mess until something workable emerges. In trying to recreate self-sustaining ecosystems, biologist Stuart Pimm says: "But keep on adding species, keep on letting them fall apart and, surprisingly, they eventually reach a mix that will not fall apart. ...It takes a lot of repeated messes to get it right."

All this messy playfulness creates relationships that make available more: more expressions, more variety, more stability, more support. In our exploration of what's possible, we are led to search for new and different partners. Who we become together will always be different than who we were alone. Our range of creative expression increases as we join with others. New relationships create new capacities.

This creative world is playful even in its processes. None of us struggles to create ourselves in isolation, fighting to survive in a world of fixed rules and unyielding circumstances. Every change we make in ourselves, every exploratory path we follow, changes many others. Our explorations even change the rules by which we change. We are not contestants pitted against one another in a game with all the rules set ahead of time. The world is more playful than this, more relational. Life invites us to create not only the forms but even the processes of discovery.

The environment is invented by our presence in it. We do not parachute into a sea of turbulence, to sink or swim. We and our environments become one system, each influencing the other, each co-determining the other. Geneticist R. C. Lewontin explains that environments are best thought of as sets of relationships organized by living beings. "Organisms do not experience environments. They create them."

This codetermination is evident in the evolution of our planet. In its nearly four billion years of experimentation, life has created Earth as a set of relationships that are hospitable to life. It has discovered both new forms and new processes. Science writer Louise B. Young describes this process beautifully:

> Life altered the atmosphere and gentled the sunlight. It turned the naked rocks of the continents into friable soil and clothed them with a richly variegated mantle of green which captured the energy of our own star for the use of living things on earth, and it softened the force of the winds. In the seas life built great reefs that broke the impact of storm-driven waves. It sifted and piled up shining beaches along the shores. Working with amazing strength and endurance life transformed an ugly and barren landscape into a benign and beautiful place.

In a universe where the desire to experiment and to create is so inescapable, it seems important to ask why. Why are novelty and experimentation so encouraged? Why does life seek to organize with other life?

When living beings link together, they form systems that create more possibilities, more freedom for individuals.

This is why life organizes, why life seeks systems – so that more may flourish.

organizing as play

Life is creative. It explores itself through play, intent on discovering what's possible. Can we bring this creative play of the world into our lives in organizations?

Life often feels like a series of tests presented to us by hostile teachers. But this isn't true. Life isn't concealing solutions to problems; we're not being tested to see if we get the right answer. Instead, life is exploring to see what works, to experience the pleasure of the unexpected and the unique.

When did opportunities begin to feel so limited? How did we come to believe in "windows of opportunity," rare openings that suddenly snap shut? When did we become so unforgiving and so punishing of one another's explorations? Experimentation doesn't use up possibilities; it creates more. More information, more experiences, more insights. We have limited the world, but it remains wide open to us.

Many of us have created lives and organizations that give very little support for experimentation. We believe that answers already exist out there, independent of us. We don't need to experiment to find what works; we just need to find the answer. So we look to other organizations, or to experts, or to reports. We are dedicated detectives, tracking down solutions, attempting to pin them on ourselves and our organizations.

Could we stop these searches? What if we gave up so much striving to discover what others were doing? What if we invested more time and attention in our own experimentation? We could focus our efforts on discovering solutions that worked uniquely for us. We could realize that solutions that are not perfect – only pretty good – can work for us. We could focus on what's viable, rather than what's right.

Observing others' successes can show us new possibilities, expand our thinking, trigger our creativity. But their experience can never provide models that will work the same for us. It is good to be inquisitive; it is hopeless to believe that they have discovered our answers.

We could give more support to our own experimentation if we focused on discovering pretty good solutions that worked for now. With more to choose from, with none bidding for support as the ultimate right answer, we might feel less attached to them. If these solutions did not require such enormous investments of resources, egos, and certainties, we could abandon them sooner when they stopped working. People could feel freer to respond creatively to the flow of events and demands, rather than feel locked in loyalty to some world-class but failing solution. Agility and the freedom to be creative are more likely when we focus on what works rather than what's right.

Discovering what works in the particular universe of any organization is the task of everyone in that organization. Most people want to dedicate their intelligence to discovering solutions that help their system work better. Life is attracted to order. People are attracted to figuring out how to make something happen. We want to be engaged in the creation of unique, daring, colorful, and surprising adaptations. We want to create for the good of our enterprises.

Playful and creative enterprises are messy and redundant. Human thinking is accomplished by processes that are messy and redundant. When computer scientists first tried to mimic the lavish parallelism found in human thinking and all of nature, they had to link together more than 64,000 computers working on the same problem at the same time. Parallel systems are dedicated to finding what works, not by careful stepwise analysis in the hands of a few experts, but by large numbers of a population messing about in the task of solution-creation. They come up with better solutions, but they are based on a different kind of logic: trying thousands of things simultaneously to find what works.

Science writer Kevin Kelly describes these systems as a "messy cascade of inter-dependent events....What emerges from the collective is not a series of critical individual actions but a multitude of simultaneous actions whose collective pattern is far more important."

Parallel systems are not afraid of error. Errors are expected, explored, welcomed. More errors create more information that results in a greater capacity to solve problems. Any one error counts for less because, while there are more of them, they are not linked together. This is not the case in the more familiar serial system, where activities build on one another in lockstep sequences and our work depends entirely on what others have done. In a serial system, one small error has the potential to crash the whole system. In the summer of 1990, America's long-distance phone service experienced frequent failures. It had taken two million lines of code to run this serial system. It took only three lines of code to bring it down.

Simultaneity reduces the impact of any one error. More errors matter less if the actors are not linked together sequentially. The space for experimentation increases as we involve more minds in the experiment, as long as they can operate independently. What links people together is their focus on a needed solution. But in discovering what works, they are not waiting for one another to act.

The simultaneity of parallel processing may look like wasteful redundancy. Yet our fears about redundancy developed from the belief that organizations work best when they mimic machine efficiencies. What is efficient for a machine – simple, stepwise operations, maximum outputs from minimum inputs, nonrepetitive parts and processes – has little correlation to the way the world explores itself. Bacterial colonies successfully locate food by sending out "random walkers." Each walker is a cluster of a thousand bacteria. Exorbitant numbers of these walkers – about ten thousand per colony – go off simultaneously, searching in all directions. Billions of years ago, bacteria discovered the real efficiency of random and redundant behaviors.

Life behaves in messy ways. It succeeds in creating, responding, and adapting by using processes that have no connection to our machine-led ways of thinking. In a living system, what is redundant? How can anyone know? Life doesn't pursue parsimony.

Fuzzy, messy, continuously exploring systems bent on discovering what works are far more practical and successful than our attempts at efficiency. Such systems are not trying to reduce inputs in order to maximize outputs. They slosh around in the mess, involve many individuals, encourage discoveries, and move quickly past mistakes. They are learning all the time, engaging everyone in finding what works. The system succeeds because it involves many tinkerers focused on figuring out what's possible.

Could we begin to appreciate that this kind of tinkering is efficient? Tinkerers make do with what is available, most often acting with fewer resources than desired. In this sense, they are extremely efficient. They experiment with what is at hand until they discover a workable solution. The solution is discovered through the doing, by noticing "the shape things will take to come forth in."

Playful tinkering requires consciousness. If we are not mindful, if our attention slips, then we can't notice what's available or discover what's possible. Staying present is the discipline of play. Great focus and concentration are required. We need to stay aware of everything that's happening as it is happening, and to respond with minimal hesitation.

Playful enterprises are alert. They are open to information, always seeking more, yearning for surprises.

The more present and aware we are as individuals and as organizations, the more choices we create. As awareness increases, we can engage with more possibilities. We are no longer held prisoner by habits, unexamined thoughts, or information we refuse to look at.

Yet we often tend to limit our explorations of what's possible by surrounding ourselves with large amounts of information that tell us nothing new. We collect information from measures that tell us how we are doing – whether we're up to standard, whether we're meeting our goals. But these measures lock us into learning only about a predetermined world. They keep us distracted from questioning our experience in a way that could create greater possibilities. They don't ask us to question why we're doing what we're doing. They don't ask us to notice what learning is available from all those things we decided not to measure.

There is an important humility associated with trying to direct our activities by setting goals or measures. Every act of observation loses more information than it gains. Whatever we decide to notice blinds us to other possibilities. In directing our attention to certain things, we lose awareness of everything else. We collapse the world of possibilities into a narrow band of observation.

In a creative organization, everyone in the organization feels compelled to be alert, seeking out new measures, new events to observe. Everyone questions whether there is more to notice. As we measure our measures, we create the conditions for much greater creativity. Our consciousness expands as we become willing to question even our processes of observation. Consciousness and creativity are inextricably linked in this always discovering world.

Living in this discovery-focused, messy, parallel-processing world can't help but engage us with the world's choice for diversity. Parallel processes require both diversity and freedom. There is more than one workable solution, and these solutions arise from many different forms of self-expression. Everyone tinkers in a unique way. No one is limited to a particular method. Everyone is free to use his or her own best thinking to discover what works.

Life is not driving us toward one solution. The world is interested in pluralism. Only in this way can it discover more about itself. As we explore our organizations' opportunities, life is calling us to experiment and change. We might discover some bold, as-yet-undreamed-of solution, some unique quirk of design or expression. When we do, we can feel pleased. But not for long. The world moves on. The world does not stay attached to a particular way of being or to a particular invention. It seeks diversity. It wants to move on to more inventing, to more possibilities. The world's desire for diversity compels us to change.

organization

the shape
things will take to come forth in

Life is attracted to order. Everywhere we look, we see life combining with other life. The universe pulses with forces of attraction that call individuals together to form more unified wholes. The history of life on our planet is a history of organization, disorganization, and reorganization. Life opens to more possibilities through new patterns of connection.

When we regarded life as a random and uninvited event on this planet, many scientists believed that the planet had existed devoid of life for most of its existence. Out of Earth's estimated four billion years of existence, life had appeared only recently in the last six hundred million years.

But recent geologic evidence reveals a very different picture. Life originated almost instantaneously with the emergence of Earth. In her pathfinding work on the microcosmic world of bacteria, biologist Lynn Margulis and science writer Dorion Sagan note: "Life has been a companion of the earth from shortly after the planet's inception." These first life forms were bacteria. Today in Norway, bacteria scraped from rocks are virtually indistinguishable from a strain of bacteria found fossilized in rocks from two to three billion years ago. Bacteria discovered how to create themselves and how to reproduce. They then spent nearly two billion years working with Earth to create a place hospitable to larger life forms. They invented the essential chemical processes of fermentation, and the use of oxygen and nitrogen, transforming a hostile atmosphere into one where life could thrive. Bacteria even invented photosynthesis.

These processes transformed the planet and made other life possible. The webs of coevolution are so intimately intertwined that we cannot understand anything in its separateness. We cannot understand the evolution of the planet separate from the evolution of the life it supports.

There is an innate striving in all forms of matter to organize into relationships. There is a great seeking for connections, a desire to organize into more complex systems that include more relationships, more variety. This desire is evident everywhere in the cosmos, at all levels of scale.

Particles are attracted to other particles and so create atoms. Microbes combine with other microbes to create capacities for larger organisms. Stars, galaxies, and solar systems emerge from gaseous clouds that swirl into coherence, creating new forms of energy and matter. Humans reach out to one another and create families, tribes, and work organizations.

Attraction is an organizing force of the universe. Everywhere, discrete elements come together, cohere, and create new forms. We know one form of this attraction as gravity. No one knows what gravity is, but it is a behavior that permeates the universe. This behavior is ubiquitous attraction.

Attraction has created the universe we know.

The tendency to organize is not just found in living beings. While it is increasingly difficult in science to distinguish the living from the non-living, few of us would categorize light bulbs as alive. Yet light bulbs have exhibited a breathtaking tendency to self-organize when wired together with other bulbs. Building on earlier work, theoretical biologist Stuart Kauffman conducted a light bulb experiment in the 1960s.

Kauffman was interested in exploring how the complex network of human genes had developed, but he used light bulbs to demonstrate that self-organization is a fundamental process found everywhere. He wired together a network of two hundred light bulbs. Each bulb was assigned a relationship with two other bulbs. It was to turn on or off based only on the behavior of either of its two assigned partners. Even with such simple conditions, the number of possible states of on and off bulbs is 10^{30}. The human imagination cannot begin to comprehend this number of possibilities. Yet Kauffman believed that the network would settle into a repeated state – a pattern of on and off bulbs. However, given such an astronomical number of possibilities, he expected to wait a very long time before a pattern of behavior emerged.

But the pattern of organization appeared instantly. After exploring only thirteen states, the system of bulbs settled into a repeatable pattern, flashing on and off in a repetitive cycle of four configurations. With a universe of possibilities to explore, the bulbs organized immediately into four patterns. Even when the connections were changed, linking bulbs to two different partners, patterns emerged, new in design, but still patterns. Organization always emerged instantly.

We live in a universe, Kauffman asserts, where we get "order for free."

We live in a universe which seeks organization. When simple relationships are created, patterns of organization emerge. Networks, living or not, have the capacity to self-organize. Global order arises from local connections. It was these cooperative structures that first created life. Life linked with other life and discovered how to continue discovering itself. Life learned how to self-organize.

Life cannot resist organizing. Self-organization is occurring all the time, everywhere. Because of this natural and innate desire to organize, life continues to explore more complex forms of organization. "I like to think that the universe is in the business of making life," says evolutionary chemist Cyril Ponnamperuma.

Anywhere we see forms and systems in nature, we see the effects of self-organization. As life organizes in response to itself, others, and its environment, patterns and structures emerge. Unlike many human initiatives, these structures are not planned or predesigned. They emerge as the system discovers what's possible. They are the result of tinkerers, not directive leaders.

For many years we have been serious students of structure. We learned to describe the forms and patterns of nature but were blind to the underlying organizing processes. Now we are beginning to understand that a deeper, more elemental force is creating these forms. We live in a self-organizing world. Structures emerge, change, disappear. New ones come into being. Each structure is evidence of life's innate desire to seek new forms of expression. Each is evidence of the innate capacity to organize.

Why does life seek to organize? Why does life choose complex relationships, dense webs that cannot be disentangled? Why hasn't life chosen simple relationships, or individuals?

Life seeks to organize so that more life can flourish. Systems are friendlier to life. They provide support and stability. They also provide more freedom for individual experimentation.

Systems emerge as individuals decide how they can live together. From such relationships, a new entity arises with new capacities and increased stability. In an ecosystem, individuals suffer less from the vagaries of weather. They may shelter and protect one another. But as a system they also moderate the climate, even changing weather conditions in their area. Individuals in systems enjoy lives of greater peace.

Yet this system-wide stability depends on the ability of its members to change. Strangely, the system maintains itself only if change is occurring somewhere in it all the time. New food sources, new neighbors, new talents appear. As conditions change, individuals experiment with new possibilities. If they fail to respond, the entire system suffers. An individual incapable of changing may disappear. Its demise will affect lives everywhere in the web.

When individuals fail to experiment or when the system refuses their offers of new ideas, then the system becomes moribund. Without constant, interior change, it sinks into the death grip of equilibrium. It no longer participates in coevolution. The system becomes vulnerable; its destruction is self-imposed.

Life requires that we change. It cannot explore new possibilities otherwise. Stable systems provide the space for our explorations. But if they do not welcome our explorations, they become rigid and die. This broad paradox of stability and freedom is the stage on which coevolution dances.

Life leaps forward when it can share its learnings. The dense webs of systems allow information to travel in all directions, speeding discovery and adaptation.

Every organism stores information in its genes. But as a process for learning, genetic mutations serve a limited role in evolution. Genetic change occurs in individuals. Benefits accrue sequentially, each waiting for the preceding one. Such individual change is far more prone to failure. If something happens to that individual, the learning disappears. The rapid evolutionary learning of life is better explained by two other processes, neither of which was clearly visible until we looked beyond survival of the fittest.

Life leaps forward by the sharing of information. Margulis and Sagan note that the world's bacteria have access to each other's information. Although bacteria developed as different strains, they never separated from one another by species-type boundaries. Virtually any bacterium can access the learning of any other bacterium. An adaptation that might take a million years if left to individual mutations can occur in just a few years because of this "global exchange network." Under stress, genes even travel between individuals; genes "jump" back and forth among bacteria with great speed. Such access to one another's learning creates incredible resiliency and adaptability. It explains why bacteria have developed such speedy, worldwide resistance to antibiotics. They operate as a "communicating and cooperating worldwide superorganism."

Life also expands and thrives by linking together. Many of us were taught that symbiosis was an interesting but unusual occurrence in life. But the opposite is true: It is the most commonly occurring phenomenon observed in living systems. "Symbiosis, the merging of organisms into new collectives, proves to be a major power of change on earth." The human body is wonderful evidence of the results of such symbiosis. Ten percent of our dry body weight is bacteria, microorganisms who linked together with us to make us possible. The vast populations that inhabit our digestive systems create an ecology that has been described as "hectic, eclectic, tumultuous." All complex organisms, Margulis and Sagan state, evolved through such tumultuous but cooperative venturing.

How can we resist noticing the forces of attraction, the willingness to link together, the capacity to self-organize? These are not absent anywhere. Life is irresistibly organizing.

It is a strange place for us to be, this self-organizing world. If order is for free, we don't have to be the organizers. We don't have to design the world. We don't have to structure existence. We don't have to struggle to create networks, affiliations, or teams. Symbiosis is not an occasional event. Organization wants to happen.

We could give up our belief that the world is falling apart, that all forms of organization are our responsibility, that it's a difficult, arduous task to create something, or to make some thing manifest. We could give up our belief that nothing happens without us.

The world knows how to create itself. We are its good partners in this process. Or we can be.

organization as organizing

Organizing is a deep impulse. The history of life is a history of organization, disorganization, and reorganization. Life opens to more possibilities through new patterns of connection.

But how many of us live and work in organizations that fulfill our desires? How many of us feel supported in our need to connect and to create? Our organizations rarely reflect our need for meaning, connection, and growth. Yet we continue to create new organizations because of our human need to be more, to do more. We notice possibilities, we notice one another, we see a need which calls us to respond, and we organize.

Can organizations learn to sustain the energy and desire that called them into being? Can organizations learn how to support us as self-organizing?

When we view organizations as machine-like objects, unavoidably they become complexities of structure, policy, and roles. We build rigid structures incapable of responding. We box ourselves in behind hard boundaries breached only by hostile forays. We create places of fear. We shrink from one another. We mistrust the elemental organizing forces of life. The struggle and competitiveness that we thought characterized life become the preeminent features of our organizations.

How many organizations believe in order for free?

Our first task, then, is to see the world differently. We need to observe processes that we either ignored or could not see. Self-organization is not a startling new feature of the world. It is the way the world has created itself for billions of years. In all of human activity, self-organization is how we begin. It is what we do until we interfere with the process and try to control one another.

We don't have to look beyond ourselves to see self-organization. Each of us has frequent personal experiences with this process. We see a need. We join with others. We find the necessary information or resources. We respond creatively, quickly. We create a solution that works.

But then, how do we describe what we did? Do we dare to describe the true fuzziness, the unexpected turns, the bursts of creative insight? Or do we pretend that we were in control every step of the way? Do we talk about surprises or only about executing plans? Do we brag about our explorations or only our predictions?

Our analytic culture drives us to so many cover-ups that it's hard to see the self-organizing capacity in any of us.

How do we support our natural desire to organize and the world's natural desire to assist us? It begins with a change in our beliefs. We give up believing that we design the world into existence and instead take up roles in support of its flourishing. We work with what is available and encourage forms to come forth. We foster tinkering and discovery. We help create connections. We nourish with information. We stay clear about what we want to accomplish. We remember that people self-organize and trust them to do so.

When we work with organizing-as-process rather than organization-as-object, it changes what we do. Processes do their own work. Our task is to provide what they need to begin their work. Do people need resources, or information, or access to new people? If they had these, could they then get on with the work? And would we let them?

This is a new way of thinking about our responsibilities. In a self-organizing system, people do for themselves most of what in the past has been done to them. Self-organizing systems create their own structures, patterns of behavior, and processes for accomplishing. They design what is necessary to do the work. They agree on behaviors and relationships that make sense to them. Those of us not directly involved in the doing of their work can give up fussing about designs, or believing that our timelines make things happen, or that our training programs change the behavior of the organization

In self-organization, structures emerge. They are not imposed. They spring from the process of doing the work. These structures will be useful but temporary. We can expect them to emerge and recede as needed. It is not the design of a specific structure that requires our attention but rather the conditions that will support the emergence of necessary structures.

Patterns and structures emerge as we connect to one another. Even simple connections lead to organized patterns of behavior. Life always organizes as networks of relationships, spinning dense webs that can't be disentangled. As we organize, we need to keep inquiring into the quality of our relationships. How much access do we have to one another? How much trust exists among us? Who else needs to be in the room?

In ecosystems, members seem to have access to the whole system. The quality of their communication is dazzling. Birds build their nests over a river at different heights each year in anticipation of the coming flood levels. Furry animals know how much snow to expect in the coming winter and dress accordingly. How do they know this? We don't know. But clearly they communicate superbly. Nothing we have created in any human organization comes close.

We do know that in healthy human systems people support one another with information and nurture one another with trust. Our wonderful abilities to self-organize are encouraged by openness. With access to our system we, like all life, can anticipate what is required of us, connect with those we need, and respond intelligently.

People don't connect with other people to accomplish less. Behind all our organizing is the desire to accomplish, to create something more. In this desire, we mimic the world. Life organizes to discover new varieties, different capacities.

But in our organizations, this organizing desire takes some strange forms. We want to generate more capacity but approach it through prescriptions and designs. We determine the levels of contribution we require and then design production roles. We try to engineer human contribution. We set clear expectations for performance. We then ask people to conform to our predictions about their contribution. We freeze them into their functions.

In a self-organizing world, this type of engineering can be described only as lunacy. Why would we seek the boxes of our predictions and cut off the expanding capacities of our colleagues? Why wouldn't we try and engage each other to evoke our creativity? Why wouldn't we plan only for unexpected levels of contribution once we were engaged in the work?

It is ironic to compare life's search for greater capacity and our own fearful designs for accomplishment. But there is another irony. In spite of our efforts to engineer and control, people around us are already self-organizing to get work done. In every organized human activity, self-organization is occurring all the time. We see it in colleagues who decide to do whatever it takes to solve a problem. We see it in times of crisis, when people pull together in unplanned and unprecedented ways.

How liberating it would be if we acknowledged self-organization. We could support one another for who we truly are.

In life, systems create the conditions for both stability and personal discovery. It's a lovely and intricate paradox. We connect with others and gain protection from external turbulence. We become part of something greater and thereby gain more freedom to experiment with ourselves. If we do not exercise that freedom to change, the organization cannot maintain its stability.

Here is another place from which to contemplate a simpler way. Stability is found in freedom – not in conformity and compliance. We may have thought that our organization's survival was guaranteed by finding the right form and insisting that everyone fit into it. But sameness is not stability. It is individual freedom that creates stable systems. It is differentness that enables us to thrive.

Self-organizing calls us to different work. It calls us to partner with the world's creative forces in a new way. We carry old perceptions of how the world works. We think that competition and domination are central. We think we struggle for our survival. But the world is systems-seeking. As we look at life through the systems of organization it loves to create, we see a world that cannot be understood well through the lens of struggle and competition.

Life seeks systems so that more may flourish. Life is in the business of creating more life. An interesting way to observe this phenomenon is in a system's creation of niches – specific areas or talents distributed with clear lines of ownership. In business, we talk about niches as a competitive strategy. We advise one another to find our unique contribution and move it into the world. We talk about the need to beat out others for our space and the need to dominate in our market. We see differentiation in nature and interpret it as the key to competitive advantage. We look at the prevalence of narrow specializations and see it as the road to supremacy.

We couldn't be more wrong. Life creates niches not to dominate, but to support. Symbiosis is the most favored path for evolution. Niches are an example of symbiosis.

Niches are created when an individual or population defines itself. Out of many possibilities, it organizes certain aspects of the environment to support its survival. In defining itself, for example, it will specify what food it needs. This declaration frees up all other food sources for others in the system. Competition is reduced by such definition. Even Darwin believed that as species explored the most efficient division of resources among themselves, competition would be diminished and nature would become "more and more diversified."

Recently, researchers have returned to the Galapagos Islands that so intrigued Darwin and observed this diversification in long-term field studies of finches. During good times, one population of cactus-eating finches shared a broad niche; they each ate from many parts of the cactus. But following a drought, birds with beaks only one millimeter longer used this slight extra length to drill into cactus fruits. Their shorter-beaked neighbors focused on fallen cactus pads that they could rip and tear. Scarcity moved them to explore more diversified ways of feeding so that they could continue to live together.

Similar symbiotic agreements are evident between very different species. If bees are absent, certain birds will seek flower nectar as part of their diet. If bees enter the system, the birds change their dietary needs and no longer look to flowers.

This process of specializing in order to remain together is difficult for us to comprehend. We have explained the world of organizing so differently. We have looked for competition and used it to explain the behaviors that we see. We believe that increased scarcity leads only to increased fights for survival. Even modern Darwinists observe the increased specialization of the finches and describe it as rooted in competition.

But living systems cannot be explained by competition. Brutal species, note Margulis and Sagan, always destroy themselves, leaving the world to those who have figured out how to coexist with one another. "While destructive species may come and go, cooperation itself increases through time."

The birds and the cacti and the bees adapt so that they can remain together. Differences that had no importance during good times become, in harder times, experiments in new ways to find food. They aren't competing to destroy one another. They are using their differences to find new ways of living together.

Evolution as survival of the fittest has inhibited our observation of coevolution. We are not independent agents fighting for ourselves against all others. There is no hostile world out there plotting our demise. There is no "out there" for anyone to occupy. We are utterly intertwined. Always we are working out conditions for life with others. We play an essential role in shaping each other's behavior. We select certain traits and behaviors. They respond to us. Their response changes us. We are linked together. We codetermine the conditions of one another's existence.

If we see life as a brutal contest among separate entities, we focus on individual contribution, individual change. This worldview not only makes us feel afraid and isolated but it also causes us to hope for heroes. If evolution is the result of changes in individuals, what we need are a few individuals who can outsmart nature and win out over the competition. Yet in a systems-seeking, coevolving world, there is no such thing as a hero. Not even a visionary leader. Everything is the result of interdependencies – systems of organization where we support, challenge, and create new combinations with others. It's hard to think about individuals at all.

We make the world lonelier and less interesting by yearning for heroes. We deny the constant, inclusionary creating that is going on; we deny our own capacity to contribute and expand.

No one forges ahead independently, molding the world to his or her presence while the rest trail admiringly behind. We tinker ourselves into existence by unobserved interactions with the players who present themselves to us. Environment, enemies, allies – all are affected by our efforts as we are by theirs. The systems we create are chosen together. They are the result of dances, not wars.

self

so that the birch tree white
touched black at branches
will stand out
wind-glittering
totally its apparent self

Life wants to happen. It calls itself into existence. Out of all information and all possibilities, an entity comes into form. An identity emerges. A self has created itself. This process of self-creation is visible everywhere. It is life taking form, creativity made visible, meaning becoming shape. It is self organization.

Self-organization is the capacity of life to invent itself. Out of nothing comes something. No externally imposed plans or designs are required. This process of invention always takes shape around an identity. There is a self that seeks to organize, to make its presence known. The desires of self set a self-organizing world in motion. Two biologists, Humberto Maturana and Francisco Varela, believe that this capacity of a self to create itself distinguishes the living from the dead. They name this process *autopoiesis* – meaning self-producing. Life began with this ability to self-produce. All living systems have this ability to create themselves, not just initially, but as the continuous process of their lives.

Because a living system produces itself, deciding what it will be and how it will operate, it enjoys enormous freedom. It is free to create itself as it desires. At the beginning, this creative expression is not bounded by any external constraints. Life makes itself up by exercising its freedom, by experimenting with different forms, by asserting different meanings. The freedom to discern and to choose lies at the heart of life. We are free to notice what we will.

This is the freedom that life gives to itself, the freedom to become. Kevin Kelly asks "Becoming what?" and then answers it well: "Becoming becoming. Life is on its way to further complications, further deepness and mystery, further processes of becoming and change. Life is circles of becoming, an autocatalytic set, inflaming itself with its own sparks, breeding upon itself more life and more wildness and more 'becomingness.' Life has no conditions, no moments that are not instantly becoming something more than life itself."

A self-organizing world is best understood by delving into its paradoxes. Life, free to create itself as it will, moves into particular forms, into defined patterns of being. Pathways and habits develop. Over time, these become boundaries, limiting the freedom of self-expression. Who we are becomes an expression of who we decided to be. Our choices become limited as we strive to be consistent with who we already are. We reference a self to continue creating a self, and that reference constrains us.

This deeply paradoxical self-referential process has intrigued humankind for thousands of years. Early Hindu sages of the Vedic tradition described self-reference as one of the five elements of spiritual practice. Carl Jung noted that the snake with its tail in its mouth – a being consuming itself – is a universal and timeless image.

Self-reference seems to be a universal process, existing at all levels of scale. Some scientists understand the existence of scientific laws as a collection of habits the universe got itself into, choosing certain modes of expression that took it down a path which led to other behaviors and other consequences. After many eons, we observe these habits as laws governing all behavior; but at the beginning, they were choices among many possibilities. "The universe," states physicist John Archibald Wheeler, "is something that is looking in at itself."

This circular process of self-reference also describes how we see the world. In their work on human cognition, Maturana and Varela explain that, at any moment, what we see is most influenced by who we have decided to be. Our eyes do not simply pick up information from an outside world and relay it to our brains. Information relayed from the outside through the eye accounts for only 20 percent of what we use to create a perception. At least 80 percent of the information that the brain works with is information already in the brain.

We each create our own worlds by what we choose to notice, creating a world of distinctions that makes sense to us. We then "see" the world through this self we have created. Information from the external world is a minor influence. We connect who we are with selected amounts of new information to enact our particular version of reality.

Because information from the outside plays such a small role in our perceptions, Maturana and Varela note something quite important for our activities with one another. We can never direct a living system. We can only disturb it. As external agents we provide only small impulses of information. We can nudge, titillate, or provoke one another into some new ways of seeing. But we can never give any-one an instruction and expect him or her to follow it precisely. We can never assume that anyone else sees the world as we do.

Their work on human cognition underscores the realization that we are all, always, poets, exploring possibilities of meaning in a world which is also all the time exploring possibilities.

Understanding that life is self-referential gives us insight into the process by which change can occur in a person, an organization, an ecosystem, or a nation. Every change is fostered by a change in self-perception. We will change our self if we believe that the change will preserve our self. We are unable to change if we cannot find ourselves in a new version of the world. We must be able to see that who we are will be available in this new situation.

Thus, we can influence each other only by connecting with who we already are. Every act of organizing occurs around an identity. Every change occurs only if we identify with it.

We encourage others to change only if we honor who they are now. We ourselves engage in change only as we discover that we might be more of who we are by becoming something different.

This process of self-creation has been explored from the beginning of thought by all spiritual teachers and, more recently, by scientists. Differentness comes into the world, a desire to be something separate. From a unified field, individual notions of self arise. This process, like all those that describe self, is enticingly paradoxical. First, something appears for which there is no known antecedent. Where does the self that is organizing originate? Or why does it attempt to separate itself from the unified field? Why does this movement toward differentiation even start? These age-old questions seem to have been left unanswered. Sages and scientists alike simply state that this is where the world as we know it originates, with the idea of separateness. Everything else follows from this first act of drawing a boundary between self and other.

As the first boundary we create, self-creation leads to a world of separations and differentness. We begin to make distinctions without which identity cannot exist. Thousands of years ago, Chinese sage Chuang Tzu said: "If there is no other, there will be no self. If there is no self, there will be none to make distinctions."

But here is another paradox. To exist, the self must create a boundary. Yet no self can survive behind the boundary it creates. If it does not remember its connectedness, the self will expire.

We misperceive the role of boundaries if we interpret them only as separations. We misperceive ourselves if we think we exist isolated from others. We misperceive the world if we see it as individuals struggling against one another.

Life coevolves. There are no separated individuals. The coevolutionary processes of life cannot support isolation. Even as we draw the boundary of self, we also are creating an environment for others to participate in. We separate ourselves, but we also create the conditions for one another's life. One self-asserting being creates itself, and its presence creates conditions for others to take form.

We find this coevolutionary process everywhere, whether we explore microbes or galaxies. Even the movement of immense continents may be possible only because miniscule sea creatures with carbonaceous shells have taken form. They and other forms of marine life may be providing the lubricant upon which tectonic plates slide past each other.

We seek out one another. Separate beings unite to create more complex beings. The separateness we thought we were creating melts into the unending dance of coadaptation and change as we become ever more aware of those from whom we cannot be separate.

Once we observe the self-creation process from a coevolutionary perspective we see that we simultaneously mold our individual identity and create a contribution to a greater whole. What we create has value only if others find meaning in us. We may be intently focused on our self and the life we are making for ourselves. We may believe we can succeed in isolation. But if our system rejects the self we have created, we are truly valueless. A self that fails to create itself as a contribution to others is irrelevant in a systems-seeking world. It will go unnoticed or rejected, lacking the sheltering stability and support that a system offers to its members. If our self-expression is not meaningful to others, we will not survive.

We cannot deny our connectedness as we build our separateness. Life does not support such a process. The boundary of self is the defining of a contribution. As such, self is an opening to connections, not a barrier behind which we fight for our survival.

When we link up with others, we open ourselves to yet another paradox. While surrendering some of our freedom, we open ourselves to even more creative forms of expression. This stage of being has been described as communion, because we are preserved as our selves but are shorn of our separateness or aloneness. What we bring to others remains our self-expression. Yet the meaning of who we are changes through our communion with them. We are identifiable as our selves. But we have discovered new meaning and different contributions, and we are no longer the same.

In a creative universe, more and more becomes possible as systems form. Beyond communion, systems offer us the possibility of becoming something different and greater than anything we had been. "Evolution is the result of self-transcendence," says physicist Erich Jantsch. We reach out beyond the boundaries of who we were and discover entirely new ways of being.

This is emergence – life exploring connections to create new and surprising capacity. Evolution results from these newly emergent capacities – where systems leap into new possibilities, where life takes new and unusual forms, where selves become more than they ever imagined. When we reach out for a different level of connection, our search for wholeness is rewarded with a world made wholly new.

Why is life engaged in self-creation? What are we observing when we see self-reference, when we see life taking new forms, playing with its freedom to be? We are observing that all life begins with consciousness. A self creating itself is consciousness made visible. A self referencing itself is consciousness in motion.

Every time we discern something as an identifiable presence, we are observing the results of another's conscious activity and using our own consciousness to observe them. Though we may not agree on what consciousness is, where it originates, or why, how else can we describe the constant self-referencing process that makes visible all we see?

It is consciousness that brings form and variety into the world. It is consciousness that joins with freedom to make life always new and surprising. Consciousness stirs us to create ourselves. Consciousness calls us to be.

selves organizing

The organizing tendency of life is always a creative act. We reach out to others to create a new being. We reach out to grow the world into new possibilities.

Every self is visionary. It wants to create a world where it can thrive. So it is with organizations. Every organization calls itself into being as a belief that something more can be accomplished by joining with others. At the heart of every organization is a self reaching out to new possibilities.

This does not mean that all intents to organize are good or healthy. Our identity may be protective and exclusionary, or dangerous to others. But every act of organizing is the expression of a self that has realized it cannot succeed alone. We organize to make our lives more purposeful. We organize always to affirm and enrich our identity.

It is strange perhaps to realize that most people have a desire to love their organizations. They love the purpose of their school, their community agency, their business. They fall in love with the identity that is trying to be expressed. They connect to the founding vision. They organize to create a different world.

We see the depths of this passion whenever an organization invites its people to create the vision of that organization. Their vision is always grander than that of the leaders; their vision always includes more of the world in its embrace.

But then we take this vital passion and institutionalize it. We create an organization. The people who loved the purpose grow to disdain the institution that was created to fulfill it. Passion mutates into procedures, into rules and roles. Instead of purpose, we focus on policies. Instead of being free to create, we impose constraints that squeeze the life out of us. The organization no longer lives. We see its bloated form and resent it for what it stops us from doing.

Too often, organizations destroy our desires. They insist on their own imperatives. They forget we are self-organizing. Sometimes, so do we.

How do we create organizations that stay alive? How do we create organizations that don't suffocate us with their imperatives for control and compliance? The answer is straightforward. We need to trust that we are self-organizing, and we need to create the conditions in which self-organization can flourish.

We live in a world where attraction is ubiquitous. Organization wants to happen. People want their lives to mean something. We seek one another to develop new capacities. With all these wonderful and innate desires calling us to organize, we can stop worrying about designing perfect structures or rules. We need to become intrigued by how we create a clear and coherent identity, a self that we can organize around.

How often do we even think about organizational identity? Or realize that it is the most compelling organizing energy available?

In organizations, as in people, identity has many dimensions. Each illuminates some aspect of who the organization is. Identity includes such dimensions as history, values, actions, core beliefs, competencies, principles, purpose, mission. None of these alone tells us who the organization is. Some are statements about who it would like to be. Some are revealing of who it really is. But together they tell the story of a self and its sojourn in a world it has created.

Identity is the source of organization. Every organization is an identity in motion, moving through the world, trying to make a difference. Therefore, the most important work we can do at the beginning of an organizing effort is to engage one another in exploring our purpose. We need to explore why we have come together. How does the purpose of this effort connect with the organization? Does it connect to our individual hopes and desires? Is the purpose big enough to welcome the contributions of us all?

Most of our organizing efforts do not begin with such a focus. We are too busy. We proliferate designs and procedures to ensure that we stay together. We focus on techniques for policing or enticing one another into behaviors and roles. We worry about timelines, accountabilities, and reward structures. Yet if we took time to ground our work in the deep connections that engage us, we would be overwhelmed by the energy and contributions so willingly given.

Whether we are beginning a relationship, a team, a community organizing effort, or a global corporation, we need together to be asking: What are we trying to be? What's possible now? How can the world be different because of us?

We can look inside any organization and find many people engaged in self-organizing. They may find themselves in a situation for which there is no prior plan or policy. They may be bothered by a problem and just decide to solve it. When they are free to act without precedents or policy, how do they respond? How do they decide which action is best?

In a self-organizing world, we all take the same route. We refer to the organization's identity. We try to identify the self that we can organize around. We use our experiences of the organization. We think about what the organization seems to value, what it has recognized and rewarded in the past.

But frequently, as we look into the organization, we see multiple selves – messages, goals, and behaviors that tell conflicting stories. How do we know what is important to the organization? Which identity should we honor? Which should we ignore?

Organizations with multiple personality disorder confuse us with their incoherence. Our innate process of self-reference breaks down. In the presence of such schizophrenia, an opportunity to choose among different selves feels too much like Russian roulette.

The only antidote to the unnerving effects of such incoherence is integrity. People and organizations with integrity are wholly themselves. No aspect of self stands different or apart. At their center is clarity, not conflict. When they go inside to find themselves, there is only one self there.

We can't resolve organizational incoherence with training programs about values, or with beautiful reports that explain the company's way, or by the charisma of any leader. We can resolve it only with coherence – fundamental integrity about who we are.

With coherence, comes the capacity to create organizations that are both free and effective. They are effective because they support people's abilities to self-organize. They are free because they know who they are.

Coherent organizations experience the world with less threat and more freedom. They don't create boundaries to defend and preserve themselves. They don't have to keep others out. Clear at their core, they become less and less concerned about where they stop. Inner clarity gives them expansionary range.

Such clarity creates order through freedom. This paradox is well displayed in the phenomenon of strange attractors. In chaos theory, strange attractors are the patterns revealed by the order inherent in chaos. A chaotic system wanders wildly, never repeating itself. Each behavior is new and unpredictable. Moment to moment the system is free to experiment. And yet there is a hidden geography to its experimentation. Something unknown calls to its wanderings and the system answers by keeping its explorations within bounds. The attractor calls the system to a certain terrain, to a certain shape.

In organizations, clear identity is an unmistakable and certain call.

As we act together in the world, our organization's identity grows and evolves. It helps periodically to question what we have become. Do we still love this organization? Do we each organize our work from the same shared sense of what is significant? Such an inquiry helps return us to the energy and passion of that space of early vision. We return to the place where our community took form, where we first became inspired by what we could be in the world. From remembering that place, together we can decide what we want to be now.

Always in that space of vision, there is passion just waiting for us to notice. People want to love their organizations. "Love," writes Catholic theologian David Steindl-Rast, "is saying yes to belonging."

When we say yes to an organization, we awaken strong responses. Steindl-Rast observes that if we agree to belong, we will feel called to new ways of living. We will notice what is required of us now that we are a community. We will act differently.

Ethics is how we behave when we decide we belong together. Daily we see this interplay of ethics and belonging in our own lives. We want to be part of an organization. We observe what is accepted or rewarded and we adapt. But these ethics are not always good. We may agree to behaviors that go against personal or societal values. Months or years later, we dislike the person we have become. Did we sacrifice some essential aspect of ourself in order to stay with an organization? What was the price of belonging?

What about those of us marooned in organizations of no belonging? Daily, we offer less and less. We withdraw our love and give it willingly to other areas of our lives.

Most people are creative and meaning-seeking. As we go through life, we don't want to become less. We need places to nurture our passions, places where we can become more. Work is one of those places. Instead of denouncing us as irresponsible, disloyal, or lazy, our organizations need to notice how they have disengaged from us. Poet David Whyte states that no organization, however large, is big enough to hold even one human soul.

Large organizations spend a great deal of time and resources on training people in behaviors under such topics as diversity, communications, and leadership. But these behaviors are not a list of rules or techniques. They arise from agreements about how people will be together. Often these agreements are unspoken. We can't train people to be open, or fair, or responsible if the real agreement is that we must succeed at all costs, or that we have no choice but to keep laying people off. Training programs can never resolve deeply incoherent messages. Neither can legislation. Behaviors are rooted in our agreements. They change only when we bring to light these unspoken commitments. Our behaviors change only if we decide to belong together differently.

Organizations can keep searching for new ties that bind us to them – new incentives, rewards, punishments. But organizations could accomplish so much more if they relied on the passion evoked when we connect to others, purpose to purpose. So many of us want to be more. So many of us hunger to discover who we might become together.

We live in a world that experiments in contrary directions. It actively encourages diverse forms of self-expression, filling the planet with variety beyond imagination. And then it coheres this diversity into systems, creating new unities from abundant variety.

This contrariness leaves us in a dilemma. We can seek the greater capacity offered to us by systems if we are willing to connect with those who feel strange, different, even deviant. Or we can barricade ourselves away from those different ones we fear, and consign ourselves to lives of separateness and deterioration. This doesn't seem like much of a choice. Yet we keep choosing separateness over systems.

The systems-seeking desire of life calls us to work with its diversity. It asks that we enrich the meaning and capacities of our organizations through our differentness. It asks that we bravely evoke with one another the deep emotions of purpose and meaning. It asks that we have faith that through differentness we can discover unifying identities.

None of this is easy. It is so different from the work we've been doing. We have identified ourselves as separate and have tried to protect ourselves from one another. We have used rules and regulations as weapons and fought to make ourselves safe. But there is no safety in separation. In a systems-seeking world, we find well-being only when we remember that we belong together.

emergence

I look for the forms
things want to come as
from what black wells of possibility,
how a thing will
unfold:

not the shape on paper – though
that, too – but the
uninterfering means on paper

Life wants to discover itself. Individuals explore possibilities and systems emerge.
They self-transcend into new forms of being. Newness appears out of nowhere.
We can never predict what will emerge. We can never go back. Life is on a one-
way street to novelty. Life always surprises us.

Emergence is the surprising capacity we discover only when we join together. New systems have properties that appear suddenly and mysteriously. These properties cannot be predicted. They do not exist in the individuals who compose the system. What we know about the individuals, no matter how rich the details, will never give us the ability to predict how they will behave as a system. Once individuals link together they become something different.

Emergence provides simple evidence that we live in a relational world. Relationships change us, reveal us, evoke more from us. We do not live in a world that encourages separateness. Only when we join with others do our gifts become visible, even to ourselves.

We witness emergence any time we are surprised by a group's accomplishments or by our own achievements within a group. We expected a certain level of behavior, and instead we discovered unknown abilities. We also see emergence vividly in the first hours after a disaster. Before official agencies can arrive, people join together and respond. Without training or direction, coordinated behaviors emerge that rescue and save. People speak about these experiences with awe and humility. They call them miracles. They remember forever those moments of extraordinary capacity that took them by surprise.

Emergence is a common phenomenon found everywhere in life. Social insects are a particularly stunning example. The tower-building termites of Africa and Australia accomplish little when they act alone; they dig only lowly piles of dirt. But as they attract other termites to their vicinity, a collective forms. As a group, they become builders of immense towers – engineering marvels filled with arches, tunnels, air conditioning systems, and specialized chambers. These intricate towers are the largest structures on earth if you consider the size of their builders. But if we observed only individual termites, we could never predict what they do as a collective. It wouldn't matter how long we observed them as individuals. The skills they have together do not exist in the individuals.

And no leader termite directs the building. All participate, doing what seems required as they observe the behavior of others. With antennae waving, they bump up against one another, notice what's going on, and respond. Acting locally to accomplish what seems to be next, they build a complex structure that can last for centuries. Without engineers, their arches meet in the middle.

Their behaviors are sophisticated, complex, and effective. Yet they arise from activities that are messy, unplanned, and nondirected. Life seeks order, but it uses messes to get there. Organizing occurs locally. Groups link up with other groups. From such small collectives, a larger system emerges. Many parallel activities, many trials and errors, are occurring everywhere in the system. Individuals determine their behavior from what they see going on around them. The result is a system so well-coordinated that it's hard to believe someone, somewhere, is not directing the activity from on high. It took entymologists a long time to realize that there were no termite construction bosses.

People organize to do more. We seek out one another because we want to accomplish something. And then life surprises us with new capacities. Until we organize, we can't know what we can accomplish together. We can't plan who we will be. Any time we join with others, newness and creativity pop up to astonish us. "The surprise within the surprise of every new discovery is that there is ever more to be discovered."

Life is playful and life plays with us. The future cannot be determined. It can only be experienced as it is occurring. Life doesn't know what it will be until it notices what it has just become.

In *The Crossing,* novelist Cormac McCarthy writes: "People speak about what is in store. But there is nothing in store. The day is made of what has come before. The world itself must be surprised at the shape of that which appears. Perhaps even God."

A system is fluid relationships that we observe as rigid structure. If we look past these structures, we see that systems spring to life from agreements among individuals on how best to live together. From this multitude of individual explorations, a system may suddenly appear. Individuals didn't know they were creating a system. They were just trying to work out the details of relating to their neighbors. But from just such local activities large systems arise, stabilized structures of new capacity.

Once the system forms, capacities can keep developing. Parents who come together to build a town playground do more than create a new park. They discover how to work together. What began as a park project transforms into relationships and shared desires that then can create more and more for the community.

This is a familiar history of community-organizing efforts. People work on a small effort and discover new skills. Their energy and belief in themselves grow; they take on another project, then another. Looking back, they see that they have created a larger system whose capacities were undreamed of when they first began.

This is how organization develops in all living systems. Local activities build on themselves – connecting, expanding, transforming – and all without traditional planning or direction. The system emerges as individuals freely work out conditions of life with their neighbors. No one worries about designing the system. Everyone concentrates on making sense of the relationships and needs that are vital to their existence. They are coevolving. From such local, autonomous, and messy negotiations, something large, complex, and useful emerges. Individual freedom leads to global stability. Through messy parallel activities, life organizes its effectiveness. It looks like a mess. It is a mess. And from the mess, a system appears that works.

When we model our organizations on standards of machine efficiency, we are told to minimize the numbers, eliminate the waste, get down to one. But an emergent world needs the messiness of many. It rewards our collaborations with systems that make more possible.

Once systems are called into the world by our individual explorations, it becomes impossible to work backwards. Systems cannot be deconstructed. We can't figure out cause and effect or who contributed what. There are no heroes or permanent leaders in an emergent, systems-creating world. There are too many simultaneous connections; individual contributions evolve too rapidly into group effects.

A system is an inseparable whole. It is not the sum of its parts. It is not greater than the sum of its parts. There is nothing to sum. There are no parts. The system is a new and different and unique contribution to its members and the world. To search backwards in time for the parts is to deny the self-transforming nature of systems. A system is knowable only as itself. It is irreducible. We can't disentangle the effects of so many relationships. The connections never end. They are impossible to understand by analysis.

If a system appears that works well, our dilemmas in understanding it through traditional analysis only intensify. The success of this system results from conditions and relations that are unique and entangled. How can we ever learn enough about them to recreate such success? Emergent phenomena cannot be recreated. They cannot be transferred. We live in a world that we cannot plan for, control, or replicate. But such an obdurate need for originality is a gift. It frees us to discover what we can become. It welcomes us into the discovery of our own uniqueness.

How do we learn to live and to create in such a world? Few of the skills we have valued maintain any importance. We have spent enormous energy attempting to plan the world into existence. We have become engineers, architects, planners, controllers, diagnosticians, leaders. We have hammered the world into the forms we wanted by paying careful attention to plans, by focusing on the steps, by assembling the right players, by supervising their behaviors. With a precise destination in mind and every step known in advance, we have studied isolated parts and assembled the best ones. We have done this with machines, with organizations, with people. We thought we could understand their capacity by studying them in isolation. We thought we could decide what we wanted and then create the world in our own images.

But we have not succeeded very well. The world is too insistent on its own processes of invention. It seeks to discover what's possible. It encourages us to tinker with new affiliations and see what works. What skills and capacities become available to us now that there is a relationship? What are we capable of now that we're together?

An emergent world asks us to stand in a different place. We can no longer stand at the end of something we visualize in detail and plan backwards from that future. Instead, we must stand at the beginning, clear in our intent, with a willingness to be involved in discovery. The world asks that we focus less on how we can coerce something to make it conform to our designs and focus more on how we can engage with one another, how we can enter into the experience and then notice what comes forth. It asks that we participate more than plan.

Emergence is so common to our experience that it's a wonder we don't recognize it, that we still believe we must plan everything into existence. How much of any human endeavor comes to fruition from precise plans unfolding step by step, just as their designers described? If we look at any successful human activity, we see that what led to success was the newly discovered capacity of people. They came together and invented new ways of doing something. They explored new realms of ingenuity. They made it happen by responding in the moment and by changing as they went along.

Our plans, blueprints, and diagrams have made it difficult to see this wonderful creative capacity growing around us all the time. We fear surprise and retreat to caution. We would rather know what's in store than be caught off guard by new possibilities.

What are we guarding against? Is newness so fearsome?

Every act of organizing is an experiment. We begin with desire, with a sense of purpose and direction. But we enter the experience vulnerable, unprotected by the illusory cloak of prediction. We acknowledge that we don't know how this work will actually unfold. We discover what we are capable of as we go along. We engage with others for the experiment. We are willing to commit to a system whose effectiveness cannot be seen until it is in motion.

Every act of organizing is an act of faith. We hope for things unseen which are true.

Very little about the emerging nature of life supports who we have tried to be. Life invites us to play along, discovering as we go. Life wants to work with us in surprising ways. We could make our lives so much more interesting, and develop so many new capacities, if we sought to work with the unknowns of emergence, rather than try and plan surprise out of our lives.

What do we do with surprise? What do we do with a world which cannot be known until it is in the process of discovering itself? It requires constant awareness, being present, being vigilant for the newly visible. We need to notice things we weren't looking for, things we didn't know would be important, influences we hadn't thought of, behaviors we couldn't predict.

An emergent world invites us to use our most human of all capacities, our consciousness. It asks us to be alert in the moment for what is unfolding. What is happening at this moment? What can we do because of what we just learned?

An emergent world welcomes us in as conscious participants and surprises us with discovery. "To recognize that everything is surprising is the first step toward recognizing that everything is gift," says Steindl-Rast.

Our plans are nothing compared to what the world so willingly gives us.

emerging organization

Do any of us truly comprehend our organizations?

If we look at our efforts to change them, we see mostly failure. For almost half a century, we've been trying to influence organizations. We still don't know how organizations change; we only know that they do. Many intelligent and good-hearted people have been involved in these quests. Our failures are not due to lack of ability or concern.

When there is so much failure in the hands of such skilled people, it can mean only that we are seeking answers in the wrong place. Collecting more details or enforcing greater rigor still won't reveal wisdom. We have to journey to a different world and see our organizations with new eyes. We have to understand that we live in a world of emergence. When we join together, new capacities always will greet us.

Emergence reveals the heart of organization, the deep processes that spin into form the systems that we see. Like any living system, every organization coevolves. Its character and capabilities emerge as it plays with possibilities. It messes about with others until a workable system appears. This system has abilities and beliefs no one planned. It accomplishes work in ways no one designed. It has relationships no one mandated.

While we worry about designs and structures, tweak procedures and rules, insist on compliance and control, we never succeed in creating an organization by these activities.

Organization wants to happen. Human organizations emerge from processes that can be comprehended but never controlled.

Because we haven't understood organizations, we have hurt one another deeply. We joined together to accomplish a purpose, we spun intricate webs of relationships, and a system emerged. But then, what happened if we disliked what emerged? How did we respond? Usually, we turned on one other. We singled out one leader, one team, a few troubling individuals. We thought that if we changed them, or got rid of them, our problems would be solved.

How many people have been terrorized by this endless search for scapegoats? For all of the terror, how often have we succeeded in changing organizations by changing individuals?

This approach to change is yet another dark Darwinistic shadow. In classic evolutionary thought, change occurs within individuals. Each of us invents our own survival strategies as we struggle against the environment. When we apply this thinking to organizations, it leads us straight to individuals. If a distasteful situation develops, or we don't like where the system is headed, we just pluck out the bad genes. We look for the mutants in our midst and expel them.

Emergent evolution explains systems quite differently. Evolution occurs in many ways, but always from the desire to work out relationships for mutual coexistence. Locale by locale, individuals and groups figure out what works for them. They exchange information; they adapt to one another; they discover symbiosis. From their efforts, a system emerges with its own identity, its own characteristics. Once the system emerges, it can't be changed by analyzing its individual members or by singling them out for removal. We can't change a system by changing individuals.

Systems are fluid relationships that we observe as rigid structures. They are webby, wandering, nonlinear, entangled messes. Because of their webbiness, they are unknowable through traditional forms of analysis. How do we draw a dynamic process? A map can't capture its complex, coevolving, self-transcending relationships. How do we dissect a process? There are no parts to understand.

Systems create pathways, communication flows, causal loops – but these all defy attempts to understand them with any precision. No matter how well we name, count, or note individuals and events, we don't get much useful information. Our skills in drawing, separating, and defining are more diversionary than explanatory when dealing with a living system.

We can't know a system until there is a system. We can't predict the system by looking at the individuals. Systems are unknowable by analysis. They are irreducible.

We can't predict the system by looking at the individuals. Yet we spend long hours analyzing ourselves as individual parts. From quick magazine quizzes to elaborate assessment procedures, we've become a culture fascinated with knowing ourselves. We want to know our styles: our learning styles, our leadership styles, our communication styles.

Many organizations use multiple assessment tools to categorize people. From such information, managers can assemble dream teams by recipe. Two of this, three of that, perhaps one renegade or intuitive to spice things up. We reassure one another that if we combine diverse styles in just the right proportions, we can cook up high-performing teams.

We don't engage in all this assessment because we are curious about the many ways people engage with life. We analyze individuals because we want to control them. We need to predict what will happen. What can we expect from this person as a leader? How will this team perform under stressful conditions? How will I handle the next crisis in my life? We fill out a form, learn our scores, and pretend that we know how life will unfold.

When we realize that the world creates newness in every relationship, we can only laugh at these studied attempts to control. We can't predict at all how we or others will perform together. We can't know ourselves in isolation. Life seeks systems. Systems are full of surprises.

Life is unpredictable. So are we.

A self-organizing system reveals itself as structures of relationships, patterns of behaviors, habits of belief, methods for accomplishing work. These patterns, structures, and methods are visible. We become entranced by their forms. We probe and dissect them down to microscopic levels of detail.

But these material forms are deceptions. They entice us to believe that we can change them by replacing one for another. If we dislike the structure of a system, we design a new one. If we are bothered by a colleague's behavior, we send him or her to training.

Yet change efforts directed at exchanging material forms have not given us the results we hoped for. We need to look past these mesmerizing effects of organization and notice the processes that give them shape. Beneath all structures and behaviors lies the real creator – dynamic processes.

Processes are not changed by focusing on their effects. Structures and behaviors are artifacts. It does no good to rearrange them. We consume a lot of time shuffling them about – redesigning the organization for the umpteenth time, rolling out a new program. But the process ignores us. It continues to produce its patterns of behavior, its structures of relationships. Or it responds to our interventions in ways we didn't expect.

There is no way to truly influence a process except to dive into its dynamics, those forces that give it life and that propel it to its present forms. Living systems take form differently, but they emerge from fundamentally similar conditions: A self gets organized. A world of shared meaning develops. Networks of relationships take form. Information is noticed, interpreted, transformed.

From these simple conditions emerge boldly different expressions of organizational forms.

A system needs access to itself. It needs to understand who it is, where it is, what it believes, what it knows. These needs are nourished by information. Information is one of the primary conditions that spawns the organizations we see. If it moves through a system freely, individuals learn and change and their discoveries can be integrated by the system. The system becomes both resilient and flexible. But if information is restricted, held tightly in certain regions, the system can neither learn nor respond.

Information feeds the local explorations that keep a system viable and stable. A new idea may appear because someone in the system reacts to information that others had ignored. Or a team changes its work based on information only they have perceived as important. With information free to move, possibilities can sprout up anywhere in the system. Each idea or solution is unique to its creator, and each one is important to the system.

No one knows what information an individual will choose to notice. This is why structuring, gatekeeping, and censoring threaten people's ability to discover something new. They also threaten the vitality and stability of the entire system.

When we shrink people's access to information, we shrink their capacity. They will still tinker to find what works. They will still invent responses. They will still self-organize. But why make this process difficult? Why starve people who want to create organization?

Systems are relationships that we observe as structures – but these relationships can't be structured. The dense webs of a system develop as individuals explore their needs to be together. Explorations are messy; what takes shape can't be predicted. Relationships spin out as individuals wander, negotiate, and discover the connections vital to their work. In this way, people create the structures for accomplishing the work of the organization.

Relationships are another essential condition that engenders the organizations that we see. The forms of the organization bear witness to how people experience one another. In fear-filled organizations, impervious structures keep materializing. People are considered dangerous. They need to be held apart from one another.

But in systems of trust, people are free to create the relationships they need. Trust enables the system to open. The system expands to include those it had excluded. More conversations – more diverse and diverging views – become important. People decide to work with those from whom they had been separate.

Systems that open to relationships also change their beliefs about information. They realize that there is greater value in circulating information than in protecting it. The system becomes focused on discovering what works. It stops defending itself from its people. Information that had been categorized as too incendiary to entrust to certain groups becomes the means for finding solutions together.

It is astonishing to see how many of the behaviors we fear in one another dissipate in the presence of good relationships. Customers engaged in finding a solution become less insistent on perfection. Colleagues linked by a work project become more tolerant of one another's lives. A community invited into a local chemical plant learns how the plant could create devastating environmental disasters, yet becomes more trusting.

These changes in attitude and behavior are not the result of any imposed program or a new company values statement. Structures and behaviors emerge from our relationships. They emerge from decisions about how to belong together.

A system lives in its own world, a world whose meaning it has made. It becomes who it is by what it has chosen to be. Every system takes form from the self it has created.

Identity, then, is another essential condition for organization. It is the self of the system that compels it toward particular actions and behaviors. It is the self that defines meaning. It is the self that invites people to change or compels them to resist.

Organizational structures emerge in response to these imperatives of identity. Identity is at the core of every organization, fueling its creation.

Rigid identities give rise to rigid organizations. Initial clarity about direction becomes hard certainty about everything. Such organizations feel unapproachable. They know the way the world works; they know who their customers are; they know the future. They stand in their certainties, suppressing disturbances, shooting messengers.

Many of us have been in these organizations and felt deeply frustrated. Why can't they see what's going on? Why aren't they listening to us? But they see through a self that admits no differences, no doubts. They don't wish to be disturbed.

Rigidly certain organizations die early. They collapse from the weight of the structures they've erected to hold themselves up. If, as individuals, we rigidify ourselves, we suffer the same fate.

But there are other organizations with identities that are clear but curious. They explore the world by understanding who they are but inquiring about who else they might be. Such inquiring organizations take form differently. They do not turn rigid. Structures are more temporary; they come and go to fit the demands of the present. Teams form for a reason, and disband when their work is finished. Relationships are not prescribed; they emerge depending on need. Information moves through the organization with its own life, sparking insight and contribution in unusual places.

Clear at their core, curious about their future, these organizations develop expansionary range.

In a world of emergence, new systems appear out of nowhere. But the forms they assume originate from dynamic processes set in motion by information, relationships, and identity. The structures that we work within, the behaviors we live out, the beliefs that we cherish can be traced back to what is occurring in these three domains. How we treat one another, how we work with information, how we develop our identity – these conditions generate all varieties of organization.

Organizations spiral into form, cohering into visibility. Like stars on winter nights, they fill our field of vision and enthrall us. But organizations emerge from fiery cores, from richly swirling dynamics. This is where we need to gaze, into the origins that give rise to such diversity of form.

motions of coherence

not so much looking for the shape
as being available
to any shape that may be
summoning itself
through me
from the self not mine but ours.

Life is in motion, "becoming becoming." The motions of life swirl inward to the creating of self and outward to the creating of the world. We turn inward to bring forth a self. Then the self extends outward, seeking others, joining together. Systems arise. Extension and desire organize into complex and meaningful forms.

Life takes form from such ceaseless motions. But the motions of life have direction. Life moves toward life. We seek for connection and restore the world to wholeness. Our seemingly separate lives become meaningful as we discover how necessary we are to each other. Meaning expands as we join life's cohering motions. Meaning deepens as we move into the dance.

Everywhere around us we see the creating motions of life. Even the rock and soil of dry desert record its history with moving waters. The earth's restlessness sits now in massive rocks once molded by volcanic bursts, glacial movement, or the planet lifting itself to new heights. "Land is a poured thing," says writer Annie Dillard. "Nothing holds; the whole show rolls."

The universe is in motion, creating more of space as energy spins off into an emptiness that becomes crowded with emergent stars.

Our children are in motion. We happily note their changes and herald them as growth. In ourselves we seem less willing to notice, but we too are in motion, evolving and changing through our lives.

Life moves, exploring and extending its space of possibilities. In constant motion, all creation discovers original newness.

These motions of life have direction. Life moves toward wholeness. It seeks coherence. This is a journey of paradox that pursues a clear direction. It is paradoxical because the path seems first to move away from wholeness to developing a self that is unique and alone. But even the creation of unique selves is an example of coherence. Every self makes sense. It creates a world and an identity that feels coherent to itself. From infinite possibilities, it chooses what to notice and how to respond. All living beings create themselves by this sense-making process of perception and response. As we look at any living being, we are observing its particular coherence, the logic it has used to create itself.

Life's movement toward coherence is more easily seen in the great energies that attract individuals into systems. Individuals extend themselves outward and create coherent networks that make more of life possible. The Galapagos finches that had slightly longer beaks brought their uniqueness into a system plagued by drought and helped neighboring birds survive. In this paradoxical way, diversity is life's means for discovering new ways of being together. Life pursues a path of differentness to a destination of wholeness.

The systems of organization that surround us – from lightbulbs to stars – glisten with new gifts. Every new system that forms is laden with surprise. These are life's blessing for moving toward others.

Life coheres into selves and systems. In its great cohering motions, life is a poet. It brings together seemingly separate elements to create and discover new meaning. Life moves, creating more of itself in the unlimitable space of wholeness.

Life wants to happen. Life is unstoppable. Anytime we try and contain life, or interfere with its fundamental need for expression, we get into trouble. Many of the dilemmas of our time arise from our inability to honor life's ceaseless urge to be and its unflappable ability to adapt.

We attempt to eliminate bacterial diseases with antibiotics and, instead, spawn bacterial colonies that render antibiotics useless. We put pesticides in fields and end up with strains of insects that thrive in the chemically charged earth. We cannot eliminate disease or blight with these approaches. Life, whatever its form, always figures out how to coevolve with our attempts at control. Life resists elimination. Life wants to happen.

It is life's irresistible urge to be that is the prevailing story of the planet. Two billion years ago, life faltered on the brink of extinction because of a dramatic rise in oxygen, a gas that was poisonous to the organisms that then existed. Oxygen wiped out these microbial organisms in catastrophic numbers. "In one of the greatest coups of all time," write Margulis and Sagan, "the [blue-green] bacteria invented a metabolic system that required the very substance that had been a deadly poison." These bacteria reacted to their changed environment and developed the process of using oxygen for respiration. They invented breathing as we know it.

Looking back two billion years, it is easy to admire this display of bacterial creativity. When it is closer to home and we experience it as resistance to our personal plans, it is more difficult to appreciate life's unstoppable search for new forms of itself. But we cannot halt life. Instead, could we be like the blue-green bacteria? Could we take what feels like threat and alter its role in our life? Could we take the boundless need to be and welcome it in as the essential energy we draw on for our endeavors?

Each of us embodies the boundless energies of life. We are creating, systems-seeking, self-organizing, meaning-seeking beings. We are identities in motion, searching for the relationships that will evoke more from us. We bring these desires to our organizations, seeking from them places where we can explore possibilities. Our energy courses through our organizations. This energy is the best hope we have for creating organizations that feel alive.

Even in existing organizations that we've designed to be fixed and rigid, the motions of coherence never cease. People are always engaged in the motions of self-creation. Self-creation either spirals inward to become smaller and more certain, or reaches out into the world to discover newness. But the desire for being cannot be stopped. Selves don't stop creating themselves.

And people are always in the motions of self-organizing. Wherever there is freedom, we reach out to respond to a problem or to make something happen. We move to organize our world so that it satisfies us more.

We are always seeking meaning in what we do. We find this in small tasks, in large causes, and in our relationships. Whatever the form, the desire to create meaningful lives is an irresistible current in all organizations.

We have been aware of these motions – but mainly because of the problems they create. We want the organization to stop moving while we figure out where it should go next. We want to move it only toward the tiny goals we set. As we try and hold everybody still until we can figure things out, the very energy that could assist us becomes a major difficulty. We try to contain people's desires to contribute rather than working with these surpluses of energy. We stop the wellsprings of effectiveness in order to boss the world around.

We have seen life's motions of coherence, but called them "change." As a field of inquiry, change has hypnotized humankind forever. Every tradition of thought, both spiritual and scientific, has sought to understand it. Western thought has depicted change as difficult and undesirable. Since life cannot be described separately from its motions, life's very energy has come to feel difficult and strangely undesirable.

In the West, people have tried to understand the world in terms of static things, machine-like structures that move on command. This line of thinking has led to some interesting ideas about change. Static objects do not possess any inherent capacity to change. They require imposed expertise and energy to move them. Change is something we do to the world, something we cause to happen.

In this world of things, change is not motion, but a description of a new state. A thing changes; change is completed when the new form is in place. Rather than understanding change as continuous, creative energy, it becomes nothing but a redesign.

Evolutionary theories have also contributed strongly to our ideas about change. Darwin's explanation of evolution created some frightening ideas because he began with the assumption that life is struggle. Change is a defense strategy prompted by struggles with external, hostile forces. If an individual can change, it may be lucky enough to survive.

It is easy to see the influence of these beliefs in our thinking today. We believe that fear is the primary motivator for change, that people change only when they are scared. We bully one another into new behaviors by telling terrifying tales of the forces that threaten us.

As a species, we continue to terrorize ourselves by these thoughts of evolution, driving ourselves toward the future by fears of being annihilated. We view life's very nature, its great creative motions, as the enemy.

We have backed ourselves into some fear-filled corners. We have come to believe that to survive, we must control everything. The world cannot be left to itself even for a moment. Fearing people, we control one another mercilessly. Fearing change, we choose our little plans over the surprise of emergence. We struggle to contain the elemental energies of life, especially people's natural desires to affiliate, to create, to contribute.

None of us would attempt to control the creating forces that bring stars into form. Why do we think human desires to bring ourselves into form are any more controllable? Or that such control is useful?

After so many years of defending ourselves against life and searching for better controls, we sit exhausted in the unyielding structures of organization we've created, wondering what happened. What happened to effectiveness, to creativity, to meaning? What happened to us? Trying to get these structures to change becomes the challenge of our lives. We draw their futures and design them into clearly better forms. We push them, we prod them. We try fear, we try enticement. We collect tools, we study techniques. We use everything we know and end up nowhere. What happened?

Yet it is only our worldview that dooms us to this incompetence. This world that we seek to control so carefully is a world we have created. We created it by what we chose to notice, by the images we used to describe what we were seeing. It was we who decided that the world was a great machine propelled by external energies. It was we who perceived the creativity of life as a dire threat. We saw life in motion and called it uncontrollable. We saw life's unending newness and called it unpredictable. We saw life's unceasing desires for discovery – we saw the dance – and called it disruptive.

Yet out beyond the shadows of our old thinking, a wholly different world appears. A world that delights in our explorations, our desires, our needs to join with others. A world that welcomes and supports our endeavors. The world knows how to grow and change. It has been doing so for billions of years. Life knows how to create systems. Life knows how to create greater capacity. Life knows how to discover meaning. The motions that we sought to wrestle from life's control are available to us to support our desires if we can stop being so afraid.

Life invites us to partner with these motions of coherence. For some this is a welcome invitation. But many of us have lived so long in contrary beliefs that we are alarmed by the suggestion. Yet none of us is a stranger to this newly seen world of motions. We, like all life, have these great creating movements in us. We are naturally suited to be partners. The invitation to join with life will restore us to the world and evoke what is best about us.

Being in a world where newness comes out of nowhere calls to our consciousness. In the presence of unending surprise, we are invited to be alert, vigilant for the newly visible. We are invited to be more present in the moment as it opens around us, less lost in reverie about plans and goals. Our attention shifts to what is happening; our skills at discernment help us focus on what just happened now.

We've thought that we are already very good at noticing things. We have inexhaustible lists of measures, procedures, and rules that keep our attention on the right things. Intent on creating futures that we desire, we keep close attention on what we want to have happen years from now. We can be so fixed on the future that we often fail to notice how things are changing around us in the present.

These careful attentions came from a different view of the world. They were rooted in our fear. We watched carefully, not to discover newness, but to avoid surprise. We watched to maintain control, not to learn how to be more inventive participants.

The call to greater awareness comes from a different place. This world of constant newness requires our consciousness. Our wonderfully human capacity for reflection and learning, though not limited to our species, is a primary contribution we make to all life. Our great capacity for learning is not for survival purposes. It is a quality of mind that we contribute to life.

The unceasing motions of the world move us deeper into entangled networks of relationships. These entanglements feel disturbingly messy. Yet messiness is simply another way of describing the freedom, surprise, and acausal nature of life's processes. Deep inside these webs, we find no easy trails between cause and effect. We can't work with these webs by striving for parsimony, neatness, or predictable efficiencies. Life leads us away from our confident determinism into systems where we are called to experiment and play rather than to predict.

Systems can't be known ahead of time. Until the system forms, we have very limited knowledge of what might emerge. The only way to know a system is to play with it. Life's restless urge to experiment and discover, its great tinkering, its wild surprises, invite us to become experimenters. Instead of defining what's right for the system and then struggling to impose it, we learn to say "Let's see."

Human organizations are not the lifeless machines we wanted them to be. We cannot instruct them with our own plans or visions. We cannot tell them what to do. Living self-organizing systems do for themselves most of what has been done to them in the past. They create responses, necessary structures, meaning. This is not a description of anarchic systems doing what they want free of all direction. It is a description of new roles for those of us who want to join in the work of the system.

Life accepts only partners, not bosses. We cannot stand outside a system as an objective, distant director. There is no objective ground to stand on anywhere in the entire universe. Our disconnection – our alleged objectivity – is an illusion; and even if we fail to realize this, the system will notice it immediately. Systems work with themselves; if we aren't part of the system, we have no potency. Systems do not accept direction, only provocation.

When Maturana and Varela noted that living systems can only be disturbed, never directed, they were defining this new role of experimenter. There is no type of *a priori* intervention that can transform the system or turn it masterfully in a desired direction. The system is spinning itself into existence. It creates itself, including its future direction and capabilities, by exercising its freedom to choose what to notice. It is not volume or quantity that stirs any system. It is interest and meaning. If the system decides that something is meaningful, it absorbs this information into itself. With lightning speed it will move information through its webs of connections, exploring and changing the meaning of the initial message. It will communicate with itself through paths we can't see. It will display connections we never dreamed of. It will take seemingly small or insignificant comments or events and explode them into large, important influences.

This is how systems behave. They leave us with no choice but to become interested experimenters, sending pulses into the system to see what it notices. We can provoke or disturb it, and then observe its responses. In this way, we learn about the system and what it is capable of doing. But even this knowledge is temporary. The system will continue to surprise itself and us with emerging abilities.

Any time we attempt to impose a solution generated by another system, any time we attempt to transfer a program from one place to another, we are not only wasting our time, we are insulting the system. Why, with its creative, discerning capacities, should it even for a moment accept a solution that is the result of another system's creativity? Why shouldn't it insist on its own insights, its own designs?

In practice, all systems do insist on exercising their own creativity. They never accept imposed solutions, pre-determined designs, or well-articulated plans that have been generated somewhere else. Too often, we interpret their refusal as resistance. We say that people innately resist change. But the resistance we experience from others is not to change itself. It is to the particular process of change that believes in imposition rather than creation. It is the resistance of a living system to being treated as a non-living thing. It is an assertion of the system's right to create. It is life insisting on its primary responsibility to create itself.

Systems create themselves and pursue paths of their own making. If we want to work with a system to influence its direction – a normal desire as we work with human organizations – the place for us to work is deep in the dynamics of the system where identity is taking form. Every being, every organization, is an identity in motion, creating itself in the world and creating its world simultaneously. The identity of a system can turn in on itself and become rigid and closed. Or the identity can move out in the world, exploring new ways of being. But always it is the process of self creation that sets organizing in motion and holds the organization to the shapes and behaviors that we see.

If we want to change what has come into form, we need to explore the self that has created what we see. All change – both individual and organizational – requires a change in the meaning that the system is enacting. It requires looking into the system's identity, the self through which it perceives and creates.

A self changes when it changes its consciousness about itself. This is true for any system – individuals, organizations, societies. As the system develops a different awareness, this changed awareness will materialize as new responses. If it fails to assign different meaning, it will maintain itself unchanged. Thus, the source of change and growth for an organization or an individual is to develop increased awareness of who it is, now. If we take time to reflect together on who we are and who we could choose to become, we will be led into the territory where change originates. We will be led to explore our agreements of belonging, the principles and values we display in our behaviors, the purposes that have called us together, the worlds we've created.

Although we get terribly distracted by the day-to-day demands of our lives, it is important to recall ourselves to the deep processes of self-making. It is important to focus our attention on the heart of our efforts. It is essential to remember that all change originates when we change our awareness of who we are.

At the heart of life's creating processes is the autonomy to create one's self. Life requires freedom. Even when systems form, they continue to thrive only if the freedom to experiment and change remains abundantly available to all system members. As we partner with life's motions and seek to create effective human endeavors, freedom and trust become paramount to our approach to organizing.

Life moves toward other life. Systems are a naturally occurring phenomenon. If we trusted more in these cohering motions, we could move into an essential role – that of supporting the system's freedom. This means supporting the system to explore new connections, new information, new ways of being. It means focusing on opening the system in all ways. And it means trusting that by doing so, the system will grow in health and capacity.

Systems become healthier as they open to include greater variety. When diversity abounds in an environment of freedom, the result is strong and resilient systems. Change can be invented anywhere and move through a well-connected system to support many others. With the finches, when one sub-species found a way to bore more deeply into cacti, it opened up a new food source. Without that invention, less food would have been available to all and many would have starved.

We can support systems in being resilient by encouraging them to exercise their freedom to explore new connections and new information. A healthy system uses its freedom to explore its identity. It is free to look outward, to bring in others, to contemplate new information. These explorations lead the system into new and different ways of being. Organizations that become more embracing of those they were defended against are always surprised at the interest and involvement they receive from these "others." If we seek our own effectiveness, we cannot help but embrace more and more of those who are connected to us in ways we refused to see.

Open and inquiring, such systems become wiser about themselves. They become more aware of their interdependencies. They no longer seek their security behind the stout walls of exclusion. They learn that by reaching out, they become stronger. Their support comes not from unnatural boundaries but from the inherent strength of wholeness.

Often our fear stops us from encouraging such openness to new connections. We become afraid that we will lose all capacity if we open our organization to new and different members, or if we reveal anything to those we have labeled as competitors. But these are just more futile attempts to hold the world still, to stop its cohering motions. In fear, we stop the energy available to us – the energy that wants to create affiliations, systems, efficacy. We restrict freedom to assert control. We choose control over effectiveness. But living systems cannot be effective if they cannot exercise their autonomy. Freedom is essential to the movements of life. It is just as essential to us and our organizations.

Partnering with life, working with its cohering motions, requires that we take life's direction seriously. Life moves toward wholeness. This direction cannot be ignored or taken lightly. People do not respond for long to small and self-centered purposes or to self-aggrandizing work. Too many organizations ask us to engage in hollow work, to be enthusiastic about small-minded visions, to commit ourselves to selfish purposes, to engage our energy in competitive drives. Those who offer us this petty work hope we won't notice how lifeless it is. They hope that life's great motions are somehow absent from us.

When we respond with disgust, when we withdraw our energy from such endeavors, it is a sign of our commitment to life and to each other. Like all life, we can pursue a direction only toward wholeness. Like all life, we learn to sidestep the fearful minds that keep us from the great cohering motions which give meaning to our lives.

"There is only the dance," wrote T. S. Eliot. There is only the dance of coherence, and it is the only dance which brings us joy.

...But follow me,

for now it pleases me to go.

The patterns of the stars are quivering
                                near the horizon now,
the north wind's picking up, and farther on
there is the cliff's edge we must reach

to start down from...

Dante

notes

6   *Whatever ancient rocks* – As quoted in Kelly, *Out of Control,* 103.

7   *It is we humans* – Prigogine, "Exploring Complexity," 102.

12   *Ezra Pound called* – As quoted in Loder, *The Transforming Moment,* 50.

13   *"I believe I experience"* – As quoted in Prigogine, "The Philosophy of Instability," 398.

13   *The key elements of this logic* – Many sources, but esp. Kelly, *Out of Control;* Levy, *Artificial Life;* Waldrop, *Complexity.*

16   *survival of the fit* – Maturana, public seminar, Seattle, December 1993, notes in our possession. See also Maturana and Varela, *The Tree of Knowledge,* chap. 5; Varela, Thompson, and Rosch, *The Embodied Mind,* chap. 9.

16   *The puzzle is how* – Varela, Thompson, and Rosch, *The Embodied Mind,* 196.

17   *A French biologist* – F. Jacob, as quoted in ibid.

17   *Biologist Stuart Pimm* – As quoted in Kelly, *Out of Control,* 95.

18   *Geneticist R. C. Lewontin* – Lewontin, *Biology as Ideology,* 109, 112.

19   *Science writer Louise B. Young* – Young, *The Unfinished Universe,* 76.

23   *Science writer Kevin Kelly* – Kelly, *Out of Control,* 21.

23   *In the summer of 1990* – Ibid., 309.

24   *Bacterial colonies successfully* – Lipkin, "Bacterial Chatter," 137.

29   *"Life has been"…Today in Norway* – Margulis and Sagan, *Microcosmos*, 72-73.

30   *We know one form* – Swimme and Berry, *The Universe Story*, 24-25.

31   *theoretical biologist Stuart Kauffman* – see Levy, "God's Heart," *Artificial Life*; Kauffman, *At Home in the Universe.*

31   *"order for free"* – Kauffman, *At Home in the Universe,* chap. 4.

32   *"I like to think"* – As quoted in Young, 69.

34   *Margulis and Sagan note* – Margulis and Sagan, *Microcosmos,* 17.

34   *It explains why bacteria* – Wiener, *The Beak of the Finch,* 257-259.

34   *"communicating and cooperating"* – Margulis and Sagan, *Microcosmos,* 17.

35   *"Symbiosis, the merging of organisms"* – Ibid., 18.

35   *Ten percent of our dry* – Ibid., 19.

35   *"hectic, eclectic, tumultuous"* – Weiner, *The Beak of the Finch,* 258.

42   *Even Darwin believed* – As quoted in Weiner, *The Beak of the Finch,* 143.

43   *Recently, researchers* – Ibid., entire book.

43   *Brutal species* – Margulis and Sagan, *Microcosmos,* 248.

47   *Two biologists* – Maturana and Varela, *The Tree of Knowledge,* chap. 2.

47   *"Becoming what?"* – Kelly, *Out of Control,* 110.

48   *Carl Jung noted* – Ibid., 124.

48   *Some scientists* – See Swimme and Berry, *The Universe Story;* Jantsch, *The Self-Organizing Universe;* Chew's "Bootstrap Theory" in physics, in Capra, *The Turning Point,* 92 and passim.

48   *"The universe"* – As quoted in Kelly, *Out of Control,* 398.

49   *In their work on* – Maturana and Varela, *The Tree of Knowledge,* 162.

51   *These age-old questions* – See Wilber, *No Boundaries,* 7 and passim; Goswami, *The Self-Aware Universe,* chap. 4.

51   *Thousands of years ago* – As quoted in Wilber, *No Boundaries,* 76.

52   *They and other forms of marine life* – Cohen and Stewart, *The Collapse of Chaos,* 424.

53   *This stage of being* – Swimme and Berry, *The Universe Story,* 71 and passim; Wilber, *Sex, Ecology, Spirituality,* 41.

53   *"Evolution is the result of"* – Jantsch, *The Self-Organizing Universe,* 183.

62   *"Love," writes Catholic theologian* – As quoted in Capra and Steindl-Rast, *Belonging to the Universe,* 57.

62   *Steindl-Rast observes* – Ibid., 16.

63   *Poet David Whyte* – Remarks at Servant Leadership Conference, St. Louis, MO., October 13, 1995, notes in our possession.

68   *The tower-building termites* – Höldobler and Wilson, *Journey to the Ants,* "The Superorganism," 107-122; see also Levy, *Artificial Life,* chap. 3; Sheldrake, *Seven Experiments That Could Change the World,* chap. 3.

69   *"The surprise within the surprise"* – Steindl-Rast, *Gratefulness, The Heart of Prayer,* 103.

69   *"People speak about"* – McCarthy, *The Crossing,* 387.

75   *"To recognize that everything"* – Steindl-Rast, *Gratefulness, The Heart of Prayer,* 215.

88   *Motions of Coherence* – The phrase comes from Ammons, "Giving Up Words with Words," *The Selected Poems,* expanded ed., 116.

89   *"Land is a poured thing"* – Dillard, *Holy the Firm*, 21.

91   *We attempt to eliminate* – Weiner, *The Beak of the Finch*, chap. 18.

91   *"In one of the"* – Margulis and Sagan, *Microcosmos*, 109.

103 *"There is only the dance"* – Eliot, "Burnt Norton," *Four Quartets*, 16.

115 *"But follow me"* – Graham, "from Dante's *Inferno,* Canto IX," in *Materialism,* 49.

bibliography

Alexander, Christopher. *The Timeless Way of Building.* New York: Oxford University Press, 1979.

Ammons, A. R. *Garbage.* New York: W. W. Norton & Co., 1993.

Ammons, A. R. *The Selected Poems,* expanded ed. New York: W. W. Norton & Co., 1986.

Ammons, A. R. *Sphere: The Form of a Motion.* New York: W. W. Norton & Co., 1974.

Barks, Coleman, trans. *The Essential Rumi.* San Francisco: HarperSanFrancisco, 1995.

Barks, Coleman, trans. *Feeling the Shoulder of the Lion: Poetry and Teaching Stories of Rumi.* Putney, VT: Threshold Books, 1991.

Barlow, Connie, ed. *From Gaia to Selfish Genes: Selected Writings in the Life Sciences.* Cambridge, MA: MIT Press, 1993.

Barlow, John Perry. "The Economy of Ideas." *Wired,* March 1994, 85-90, 126-129.

Bateson, Gregory. *Steps to an Ecology of Mind.* New York: Ballantine Books, 1972.

Bell, Daniel. *Work and Its Discontents.* New York: League for Industrial Democracy, 1970.

Bohm, David. *Wholeness and the Implicate Order.* London: Ark Paperbacks, 1980.

Bohm, David, and Mark Edwards. *Changing Consciousness: Exploring the Hidden Source of the Social, Political and Environmental Crises Facing Our World.* New York: Harper-San Francisco, 1991.

Bronowski, J. *The Common Sense of Science.* Cambridge, MA: Harvard University Press, 1978.

Brown, Kenneth A. *Cycles of Rock and Water: At the Pacific Edge.* New York: HarperCollins, 1993.

Capra, Fritjof. *The Turning Point: Science, Society and the Rising Culture.* Toronto: Bantam, 1982.

Capra, Fritjof, and David Steindl-Rast. *Belonging to the Universe: Explorations on the Frontiers of Science and Spirituality.* New York: HarperSanFrancisco, 1991.

Cohen, Jack, and Ian Stewart. *The Collapse of Chaos: Discovering Simplicity in a Complex World.* New York: Viking, 1994.

Darwin, Charles. *The Origin of Species.* New York: W. W. Norton and Co., 1975.

Davies, Paul. *The Cosmic Blueprint: New Discoveries in Nature's Creative Ability to Order the Universe.* New York: Touchstone, 1988.

Dawkins, Richard. *The Extended Phenotype: The Long Reach of the Gene.* Oxford: Oxford University Press, 1982.

Dillard, Annie. *Holy the Firm.* New York: Harper & Row, 1977.

Dobbs, Betty Jo Teeter, and Margaret C. Jacob. *Newton and the Culture of Newtonianism.* Atlantic Highlands, NJ: Humanities Press, 1995.

Eldredge, Niles. *Reinventing Darwin: The Great Debate at the High Table of Evolutionary Theory.* New York: John Wiley & Sons, 1995.

Eliot, T. S. *Four Quartets.* San Diego: Harcourt Brace Jovanovich, 1943.

Ferris, Timothy. *Coming of Age in the Milky Way.* New York: Anchor Books, 1988.

Graham, Jorie. *Materialism.* Hopewell, NJ: The Ecco Press, 1995.

Goswami, Amit, with Richard E. Reed and Maggie Goswami. *The Self-Aware Universe: How Consciousness Creates the Material World.* New York: G. P. Putnam's Sons, 1993.

Gould, Steven Jay. *Ever Since Darwin: Reflections in Natural History.* New York: W. W. Norton & Co., 1974.

Gregory, Bruce. *Inventing Reality: Physics as Language.* New York: John Wiley & Sons, 1988.

Guenther, Herbert V. *Wholeness Lost and Wholeness Regained: Forgotten Tales of Individuation from Ancient Tibet.* Albany: State University of New York Press, 1994.

Hare, Tony, ed. *Habitats.* New York: Macmillan USA ,1993.

Hayles, N. Katherine. *Chaos Bound: Orderly Disorder in Contemporary Literature and Science.* Ithaca, NY: Cornell University Press, 1990.

Hayles, N. Katherine. *The Cosmic Web: Scientific Field Models and Literary Strategies in the 20th Century.* Ithaca, NY: Cornell University Press, 1984.

Hayward, Jeremy W., and Francisco Varela. *Gentle Bridges: Conversations with the Dalai Lama on the Sciences of Mind.* Boston: Shambala, 1992.

Hölldobler, Bert, and Edward O. Wilson. *Journey to the Ants: A Story of Scientific Exploration.* Cambridge, MA: Belknap Press, 1994.

Holland, John H. *Hidden Order: How Adaptation Builds Complexity.* Reading, MA: Addison-Wesley Publishing, 1995.

Illich, Ivan. *Medical Nemesis: The Expropriation of Health.* New York: Pantheon Books, 1976.

Jantsch, Erich. *The Self-Organizing Universe: Scientific and Human Implications of the Emerging Paradigm of Evolution.* London: Pergamon, 1980.

Jung, C. G. *Memories, Dreams, Reflections,* edited by Aniela Jaffe. New York: Vintage Books, 1963.

Kauffman, Stuart. *At Home in the Universe: The Search for the Laws of Self-Organization and Complexity.* New York: Oxford University Press, 1995.

Kauffman, Stuart. *The Origins of Order: Self-Organization and Selection in Evolution.* Oxford: Oxford University Press, 1993.

Keller, Evelyn Fox. *Refiguring Life: Metaphors of Twentieth-Century Biology.* New York: Columbia University Press, 1995.

Kellert, Stephen H. *In the Wake of Chaos: Unpredictable Order in Dynamical Systems.* Chicago: University of Chicago Press, 1993.

Kelly, Kevin. *Out of Control: The Rise of Neo-Biological Civilization.* Reading, MA: Addison-Wesley, 1994.

Levy, Steven. *Artificial Life.* New York: Vintage Books, 1992.

Lewin, Roger. *Complexity: Life at the Edge of Chaos.* New York: Macmillan, 1992.

Lewontin, R. C. *Biology as Ideology: The Doctrine of DNA.* New York: HarperCollins, 1991.

Lipkin, Richard. "Bacterial Chatter," *Science News,* March 4, 1995, 137.

Loder, James E. *The Transforming Moment,* 2d ed. Colorado Springs: Helmer & Howard, 1989.

Losee, John. *Philosophy of Science,* 3rd ed. Oxford: Oxford University Press, 1993.

Lovelock, J. E. *The Ages of Gaia: A Biography of Our Living Earth.* New York: W. W. Norton, 1988.

Lovelock, J. E. *Gaia: A New Look at Life on Earth.* Oxford: Oxford University Press, 1979.

Mansfield, Victor. *Synchronicity, Science and Soul-Making.* Peru, IL: Open Court Publishing, 1995.

Margulis, Lynn, and Dorion Sagan. *Microcosmos: Four Billion Years of Evolution from Our Microbial Ancestors.* New York: Summit Books, 1986.

Maturana, Humberto R., and Francisco J. Varela. *The Tree of Knowledge: The Biological Roots of Human Understanding.* Boston: Shambala, 1992.

Mayr, Ernst. *Toward a New Philosophy of Biology: Observations of an Evolutionist.* Cambridge, MA: Harvard University Press, 1988.

McCarthy, Cormac. *The Crossing.* New York: Alfred A. Knopf, 1994.

Mitchell, Steven, trans. *The Tao Te Ching.* New York: HarperCollins, 1988.

Palmer, Parker J. *The Active Life: Wisdom for Work, Creativity and Caring.* San Francisco: Harper and Row, 1990.

Palmer, Parker J. *To Know as We Are Known: A Spirituality of Education.* San Francisco: Harper and Row, 1983.

Prigogine, Ilya. "Exploring Complexity." *European Journal of Operational Research* 30 (1987): 97-103.

Prigogine, Ilya. *From Being to Becoming: Time and Complexity in the Physical Sciences.* New York: W. H. Freeman and Co., 1980.

Prigogine, Ilya, and Isabelle Stengers. *Order Out of Chaos: Man's New Dialogue with Nature.* New York: Bantam Books, 1984.

Prigogine, Ilya. "The Philosophy of Instability." *Futures,* August 1989, 396-400.

Rosenfield, Israel. *The Invention of Memory: A New View of the Brain.* New York: Basic Books, 1988.

Ruse, Michael. *The Darwinian Paradigm: Essays on Its History, Philosophy, and Religious Implications.* London: Routledge, 1989.

Sacks, Oliver. *An Anthropologist on Mars: Seven Paradoxical Tales.* New York: Alfred A. Knopf, 1995.

Sheldrake, Rupert. *A New Science of Life: The Hypothesis of Causative Formation.* Los Angeles: Jeremy Tarcher, 1981.

Sheldrake, Rupert. *The Presence of the Past: Morphic Resonance and the Habits of Nature.* New York: Vintage Books, 1988.

Sheldrake, Rupert. *The Rebirth of Nature: The Greening of Science and God.* New York: Bantam Books, 1991.

Sheldrake, Rupert. *Seven Experiments That Could Change the World: A Do-It-Yourself Guide to Revolutionary Science.* New York: Riverhead Books, 1995.

Schrage, Michael. *Shared Minds: The New Technologies of Collaboration.* New York: Random House, 1990.

Steindl-Rast, Brother David. *Gratefulness, the Heart of Prayer: An Approach to Life in Fullness.* New York: Paulist Press, 1984.

Swimme, Brian, and Thomas Berry. *The Universe Story: From the Primordial Flaring Forth to the Ecozoic Era – A Celebration of the Unfolding of the Cosmos.* San Francisco: HarperSanFrancisco, 1991.

Thomas, Lewis. *The Lives of a Cell: Notes of a Biology Watcher.* Toronto: Bantam Books, 1974.

Thompson, William Irwin, ed. *Gaia, A Way of Knowing: Political Implications of the New Biology.* New York: Lindisfarne Press, 1987.

Thompson, William Irwin, ed. *Gaia 2: Emergence: The New Science of Becoming.* New York: Lindisfarne Press, 1991.

Turbayne, Colin. *The Myth of Metaphor.* New Haven, CT: Yale University Press, 1962.

Varela, Francisco, Evan Thompson, and Eleanor Rosch. *The Embodied Mind: Cognitive Science and Human Experience.* Cambridge, MA: MIT Press, 1991.

Waldrop, Mitchell. *Complexity: The Emerging New Paradigm at the Edge of Order and Chaos.* New York: Simon and Schuster, 1992.

Weiner, Jonathan. *The Beak of the Finch: A Story of Evolution in Our Time.* New York: Alfred A. Knopf, 1995.

Weisbord, Marvin. *Productive Workplaces: Organizing and Managing for Dignity, Meaning, and Community.* San Francisco: Jossey-Bass Publishers, 1988.

Wesson, Robert. *Beyond Natural Selection.* Cambridge, MA: MIT Press, 1991.

Wheatley, Margaret J. *Leadership and the New Science: Learning about Organization from an Orderly Universe.* San Francisco: Berrett-Koehler, 1992.

White, Michael, and John Gribbin. *Darwin: A Life in Science.* New York: Dutton, 1995.

Whyte, David. *The Heart Aroused: Poetry and the Preservation of the Soul in Corporate America.* New York: Doubleday, 1994.

Wilber, Ken. *No Boundaries: Eastern and Western Approaches to Personal Growth.* Boston: Shambala, 1979.

Wilber, Ken. *Sex, Ecology, Spirituality: The Spirit of Evolution.* Boston: Shambala, 1995.

Young, Louise B. *The Unfinished Universe.* New York: Oxford University Press, 1986.

Zohar, Danah, and Ian Marshall. *The Quantum Society: Mind, Physics, and a New Social Vision.* New York: William Morrow & Co., 1994.

index

A

abilities, and emergence, 98
access, need for, 38-39, 82
accomplishment, in a group, 67, 69, 81
accountability, 59
adaptation, 33, 78
alertness/attentiveness, 25-26, 47, 49, 75, 95-96, 98. *See also* consciousness
altruism. *See* helpfulness
Ammons, A. R., 9
analysis, limitations of, 37, 72-74, 79-81
assessment tools, 80
attitudes, and change, 84, 91
attraction and order, 30, 35, 58, 90
autopoiesis, 47
awareness. *See* consciousness

B

bacteria, examples from, 24, 29, 33, 35, 52, 91
bees, examples from, 43
behavior, in organizations, 81, 84, 87
being present, 25-26
beliefs
    about organizations, 2-3, 37, 42

importance of, 35, 38, 44, 58, 81-82, 87, 92-96
belonging, and organizations, 62-63, 84, 87, 100
Bergson, Henri, 13
birds, examples from, 39, 43
boundaries, creation of, 48, 51, 53, 61, 64
brain, and information, 49
bravery, and meaning, 64
bricolage, 17. *See also* tinkering.

C

cactus, 43, 101
capacity, in systems, 74-75, 95
cause and effect, 97
causes, and meaning, 92
censoring, and information, 82
change
    characteristics of, 13-14, 27, 33, 41, 74, 81, 93, 100-101
    images of, 93
    in organizations, 50, 78, 81, 98, 100
    process of, 50-52, 82, 89, 99

101-102
 examples of, 16, 43
 in organizations, 63, 87
domination, 42
dynamic processes, 81, 87

E

ecosystem, 17, 39, 50
effectiveness, conditions for, 60, 94,
 101-102
efficiency, 13, 24, 97
Eliot, T. S., 103
emergence, 53, 66-87
energy
 as characteristic of life, 62, 70, 73, 89, 93
 and fear, 94, 102
 in systems, 36, 59, 92
engagement, and emergence, 73
engineering, as control, 40, 73
environment, and relationships, 18, 19
equilibrium, as death, 33
error, role of, 22-24
ethics, in organizations, 62
evolution, 19, 42, 44, 53, 62, 78, 89, 93-94.
 See also coevolution.
experimentation, as characteristic of life,
 13-14, 19-22, 24, 33, 47, 64, 74, 97-98
exploration
 as characteristic of life, 37, 49, 82, 86, 89,
 101
 in systems, 25, 83, 95, 98, 101
 punishment of, 20

F

failure, in organizations, 22, 76-77
faith, and organization, 74
fear
 as approach to life, 5-6, 11, 16, 64, 84, 96,
 103
 as motive for change, 93-95

in organizations, 15, 22-23, 37, 74, 78,
 83, 102
fermentation, invention of, 29
finches, in Galapagos Islands, 43, 90, 101
form, creation of, 41, 48, 54, 60, 81, 83, 85,
 87, 92, 94. *See also* emergence.
freedom
 characteristics of, 9, 41, 47, 61, 92, 97
 in systems, 19, 33, 98, 101
 need for, 41, 53-54, 101-102
fuzziness, as characteristic of life, 13, 25,
 37

G

Galapagos Islands, 43, 90
galaxies, 52
gatekeeping, 82
gene-sharing, among bacteria, 33
genetic change, 33
geology, examples from, 6, 29, 89
global achievements, 32, 70-71
goals, in organizations, 26, 92, 96
gravity, as attraction, 30

H

habits, creation of, 26, 48, 81
health, in organizations, 39, 56-64, 101-102
helpfulness, as human characteristic, 23, 40,
 67
heroes, 44, 72
Hinduism, 48
history, in organizations, 58
hope, in organizations, 74, 92
hospitality, of planet to life, 19, 29
hostility
 as worldview, 11, 20, 44, 94
 in organizations, 36-37, 78, 93, 101
human biology, and symbiosis, 35
human nature, optimism about, 5-6, 40
humility, 26, 67, 78

healthy, 38-39, 74, 78
influences on, 22, 33, 49, 52, 100
self-organizing, 81-87
spontaneity in, 19, 30, 42, 47, 79-80, 101

T

techniques, of control, 63, 94
telephone service, 1990 crash of, 23
termites, 68
threats, attitudes toward, 61, 91, 93, 95
timelines, 38, 59
tinkering, as approach to problems, 10, 17,
    25, 27, 32, 38, 44, 73, 97, 82
training, as control, 38, 60, 63, 81
transcendence, 71
trial and error, 68
triviality and work, 103
trust, in organizations, 38-39, 58, 83-84, 101
Tzu, Chuang, 51

U

unified field, 51
unpredictability, of systems, 67, 76-80, 83,
    95, 97

V

values, in organizations, 58, 60, 62, 84, 100
Varela, Francisco, 47, 49, 98
variety, 18, 64, 101
Vedic tradition, 48
vision, for organizations, 56-57, 61-62, 73,
    76, 97, 103

W

war, as metaphor, 44
webs, of relationships, 33, 39, 79, 83, 97-98
Wheeler, John Archibald, 48
wholeness, 53, 88, 90, 103
Whyte, David, 63
windows of opportunity, belief in, 13, 20
withdrawal, 103
worldviews, influence of, 1-3, 11, 37, 42-44,
    95-96

Y

Young, Louise B., 19

the authors

Since 1976, the two of us have been friends, colleagues, and partners in an evolving inquiry into the nature of life and organizations. *Leadership and the New Science,* Meg's award-winning and best-selling book, marked a clear new path for this phase of our inquiry. We continue to think and work together through two different organizations. The first is our consulting and education firm, Kellner-Rogers & Wheatley Inc. The second is The Berkana Institute, a not-for-profit foundation we created in 1991 to develop communities of support and inquiry focused on discovering the new ideas and new forms that represent the future of organizing. As we look back at our history together, we note that the questions we pursue and the beliefs we hold have emerged from a web of entangled events, people, and experiences over the last two decades.

We are grateful that we received good educations and learned early in life that thinking was exciting and useful work. Meg has a strong liberal arts background that includes work in science, history, literature, systems thinking, and organizational theory. She studied at the University of Rochester, University College London, New York University, and Harvard, where she received a doctorate in Administration, Planning and Social Policy. She also served two years in Korea in the Peace Corps, and worked for five years as an educational administrator before moving on to the diverse worlds of corporations and academe.

Myron credits his early education at Xavarian and Jesuit institutions for his passion for thought. His education includes work in economics, literature, and theater at Holy Cross, Tufts University, and the University of Massachusetts.

Our consulting careers began twenty years ago in Cambridge, Massachusetts. We consulted to a wide variety of institutions, at all levels, and carried out research on how organizational structures and systems impacted individual behaviors. In 1989, Meg moved west to join the faculty of the Marriott School of Management at Brigham Young University. During this period, Myron was a senior executive in retail, manufacturing, and marketing organizations. He developed expertise on issues of international organization and business development.

Since 1990, we have explored the emerging self-organizing paradigm and its implications for how we organize our work and our lives. Through our consulting, we work with a startlingly broad range of organizations, from public schools to the U.S. Army, from health care to high technology, from communities to global corporations. We also speak frequently to similarly diverse audiences in the U.S. and abroad, and we hold public seminars on self-organization in the mountains of Utah at Sundance Resort, a place that continues to inspire us and those who come there.

The Berkana Institute is an important source of new ideas and new friends for us. For several years, we have held dialogues with people from all types of communities, countries, and organizations. Together we have developed new ideas and helped one another feel less crazy for thinking such radical thoughts and holding such bold dreams. We have learned a great deal from one another and are very grateful for the ideas and support that continue to be generated from the Berkana community.

We can be reached at: Kellner-Rogers & Wheatley Inc., P.O. Box 1407, Provo, Utah 84603 Phone: 801-377-2996 Fax: 801-377-2998